# FOR  WORTH

## Thoughts of a Spiritual Curmudgeon

*SELECTED ESSAYS 1995–2006*

### RICHARD GRESSLEY

**Photographs by Barbara W. Carlson**

*for Mark ~
for me to offer this
to you may seem like hubris,
but it's really an act of
deep admiration.
— Rich*

**Bookstand Publishing**
www.BookstandPublishing.com

Published by
Bookstand Publishing
Houston, TX 77079
2951_3

ISBN 978-1-58909-664-6

Printed in the United States of America

# Table of Contents

# INTRODUCTION

Who'd have thought it would ever come to this? People often utter this in despair over some calamity. Here, I say it in awe at this realization of one of my grandest dreams. Since childhood, I've admired writers – those learned people who had recorded enough of their own thoughts, literally, "to fill a book." I never thought that I could accomplish such an Olympian thing. These years later, when I had, indeed, accumulated enough short essays to constitute a book, I hadn't the slightest idea how one gets a book published. Two men, great friends to me, undertook this task and this volume is the result of their efforts.

These essays were written for the monthly newsletter of my church, the Shoreline Unitarian Universalist Society (hereafter referred to in the text as SUUS), in Madison, Connecticut, and they are reflections of my religion. I realize that "religion" is one of the most controversial words spoken in our world today, and I hope that no one who has just encountered it here will now toss the book away. I am comfortable in my Unitarian Universalist (hereafter abbreviated as UUism, and its adherents as UUs) faith solely because it has no creed, no sacred figures to be worshiped, and requires no confession of doctrinal beliefs from me. Great theological mysteries, such as the existence of God and life after death, are up to me to decide upon to the best of my abilities. It has been described as a religion from which no one can be excommunicated save by the death of goodness in their own breast. I regard UUism not as set of rituals and recitations, but rather as a perspective on and a way of living my life on this Earth each day.

The newsletter column, also called "For What It's Worth," came about as a result of a committee report I once delivered at SUUS. Member Barbara Carlson, a journalist and author, thought it had enough catchy turns of phrase for her to cajole me into trying to write something – anything – regularly for the newsletter. She put no restraints on what I could write about, which resulted in my scattershot eclecticism. Quite to my own disbelief, I wrote my first piece well over a decade ago and am still sweating to come up with a new one each month.

I am first to acknowledge that I have no degree or formal training in writing, but I know whom I like. I hope it doesn't sound like ludicrous overreach to say that I stand in greatest admiration of Herman Melville (who, incidentally, attended a Unitarian church in 19th-century New York City). Ishmael's penchant for equating quotidian events in his own life with the great events of history and themes of the Universe ("With a philosophical flourish, Cato throws himself upon his sword; I quietly take to the ship.") greatly appeals to me for I do believe that each of our lives is lived as our own variation of these events and themes. I also admire Emily Dickinson and Ralph Waldo Emerson (himself a onetime Unitarian minister) for their concise expression of profound things, though, I confess, completely understanding them taxes me frequently! What humor may come through these essays I credit to my admiration of the droll understatement of Calvin Trillin and NPR commentator David Bouchier.

Many thanks go to my friends at SUUS, whose enthusiastic and supportive comments to me about these essays enabled me to persevere in writing them. My great and deep gratitude goes to those aforementioned friends, Dick Bastian and Fred Struve, who thought enough of my efforts to take upon themselves the considerable chore of publishing this book. In this endeavor they were supported in spirit by the SUUS Board of Trustees, to whom much credit is also due. My gratitude also to proofreading nitpicker Barbara Carlson for enabling this to be an illustrated and relatively typo-free book. Final and vital thanks go to my former partner, Nancy Ford, and especially to Helen Kennedy, without whose patience and guiding hands on the mouse, these things would never have seen the light of the computer screen.

R.G.

January, 2009
Guilford, Connecticut

# THE MAN I MET

I took a short walk around my block before work the other day. I'm fortunate that my block is no Levittown "American Beauty" suburban tract. Instead, a sidewalk-less road meanders down along a brook to a small lake, then up a short, cardiovascular-challenging hill. At the top of the hill, overhanging tree branches intertwine over the road,  turning that stretch into a tunnel. The dark aspect of this idyll is that my addictive personality turned Monday's diversion into Wednesday's habit, then Friday's rigid obligation. Happily, in this spring, the journey's pleasures outweighed the compulsion. The colors and calls of ordinary robins and jays diverted me. Winter's bare branches were now bursting white, pink and purple, and each May astonishes me again at how many different shades green comes in.

Normally on this early morning stroll, I'm as alone as Adam in Eden, but one morning, as I entered the road-tunnel, I saw at the far end and coming toward me not Eve but...another Adam. This second Adam was not totally unknown to me. Often during my couch-potato morning reading time, I had seen him through my living room window. A regular exerciser, he was, I guessed, in his seventies, and from his severe, set face I'd snap-judged that he was crotchety and unpleasant, a man I was happy not to encounter. But now, here I was striding his route from the opposite direction and in fifty more steps we'd be face to face.

Acknowledge? Ignore? In fifty paces my discomfiture had no time to come to a rolling boil – nor, as it happened, did it need to. As we passed each other, the man's eagle stern eyes softened and a smile rounded off his craggy features. "Good morning," he said gently. "Ah…good morning," I responded, as much surprised as pleased. Suddenly, advocacy replaced apprehension and now everything was new. On a small scale, it was like some first flush of love.

Stepping off the next day, I anticipated not birds and blossoms, but what best to say to build on our positive first encounter. This man now *mattered* to me and I wanted to prove myself worthy by rising above "nice weather" clichés; I needed to utter something pithy and elegant. But, I countered, I don't really know this person at all. Suppose he comes at me with something like, "Hey, how 'bout those Mets, huh?" I don't even know whether the Mets are in the American League or the National League.

Top of the hill, into the branch tunnel and along he came. As we passed this time, the eyes again softened, the smile reappeared and he said, "Everything smells so fresh this time of year." Ooohh! Positively Thoreauvian ! A kindred, cherished soul. Now how could I match his eloquence on our next pass-by? Some one-liner seemed insufficient. I wanted to stop with him in the middle of the road and have a long transcendental discussion about walking and nature and mindfulness and Life. But I also recognized my tendency to plunge immediately off the deep end. In reality, what we were both about was perambulation, not discourse.

Subsequent mornings, we exchanged just hellos and observations on how warm or chilly it was. I realized this was only proper. Maybe someday I'd run into him while

2

buying milk or a newspaper, and then would be the time for names and finding out. Or perhaps not. I pondered The Lesson from all this. Certainly it was another cautionary tale about the danger of snap – even *any* – judgments. But the moral involved more than simply judgmentalism. I considered the effect my new acquaintance had on me. To have just one stranger, out of scores we encounter daily, go from being an object of indifference (or worse) to being the subject of kind contemplation is some small holy thing.

Only connect, indeed.

# GRACE IS GRAVY

Each year, just as autumn chills down the air and most flowers are dying, my bunker mentality comes into full bloom. As the thermometer drops, my physique adopts an atavistic, hunched-over stance. This "keep warm" clench, this Nature-as-adversary regard inhabits not only my body, but also my entire worldview.

Thus driving to work one recent frosty morning, I found myself increasingly crouched defensively over the steering wheel. Rounding a curve, I noted with foreboding the heavy sweater on a woman leaving letters for pickup in her roadside mailbox. But then, shortly beyond, in front of a stand of trees, I beheld two young deer. Half again as big as Great Danes, they stood on twig legs; their large, dark eyes watched me with (what I interpreted as) a mix of anxiety and curiosity.

Immediately I sat up out of my crouch and the washboard wrinkles in my forehead relaxed smooth. My scowl inverted into a smile and I whispered a low "wow" to myself. I braked my car to a crawl, in part lest they suddenly bolt in front of me, but as much to prolong my witness of two large and supple creatures infrequently seen. After slowly rolling past them, I reluctantly accelerated, still glancing back in my rearview mirror. I saw the mail depositor's car slow suddenly and I hoped that she too was experiencing a few moments of grace.

Whoa – grace? Where did *that* word come from? It time machined me back to Protestant Sunday School when I was nine, and it, along with "sin," remains on a list of words that make me squirm to this day. Over these many years, I've preferred an earthier g-word used once by a writer who was seriously ill and given mere months to live.

He survived more than a decade and said, "I've had ten more years than I expected...gravy."

What chafes my brain about "grace" is its dictionary definition as "an excellence granted by God; an unmerited gift from God." I think this perpetuates assumptions I feel are, shall I say, unhelpful. It taxes my credulity to accept that of all the untold billions of worlds in this Universe, God singles out this minute speck to occasionally sprinkle here and there, on this one or that, little goodies. Further, the notion that such gifts are "unmerited" connotes traditional religion's view that humans are unworthy sinners. UUs, by contrast, anchor their faith on a principle of every person's dignity and worth.

Grace – gravy – is not rationed out by the occasional teaspoon; it is lavished upon this world by the ladleful. Recalling the thought that we walk unheedingly amidst miracles, I could have been just as moved by a blade of grass or a mosquito as I was by the deer. Thomas Paine (giving the lie to Theodore Roosevelt's smear, "that filthy little atheist") said, "...do we want to know what God is? Search not the book called the Scripture, which any human hand might make, but the Scripture called Creation."

Whether God made this Creation, and whether we humans "merit" its abundance, I believe are (so far) unanswerable questions. I espouse what biologist Ursula Goodenough calls "religious naturalism – a profound appreciation of the...natural world in all of its staggering, interdependent splendor." The very existence, the intrinsic "is-ness" of this vast Universe we inhabit, is its own reason for wonder and awe. As Keats said about the truth and beauty of that ancient jug, that is all you know and all you need to know.

# JUST ONE MORE

Lately, it seems as if the bearded gent who paces the sidewalk in robe and sandals has been holding his sign right up to my face. And his famous plaque reads, "The End is Near." Since beginning a hectic new job, I have been assured by SUUS leaders and laity that it would be perfectly okay to put "For What It's Worth" on hold for a while (as I have reluctantly done with some volunteer activities), and even exercise in the future the "do not resuscitate" option. There is an appeal in this proposition. Last summer, when I reached the ten-year mark in writing these things, I felt I had reached – somewhat out of breath – a finish line of sorts.

Now, my new job is full-time, with regular evening and all-weekend hours. Each shift is a blur of activity, not unlike sticking your head in a cement mixer. And to think that one of my early therapists, way back when (1966), counseled that my "career" should consist of "some low-pressure job somewhere." I do rather picture myself as being of kindred mind with the congressman once disparaged by President Lyndon Johnson as unable to "walk and chew gum at the same time." To defend myself, I cite the Buddhist tale of the wise village elder who, as he sat on the river bank fishing, was approached by the townspeople and asked to be their mayor. He declined because, "right now I am fishing." One enterprise at a time to which to devote one's complete attention and effort. To eliminate one multitasking (bad concept, horrid word) effort definitely has its attraction ... and yet ... here I am, writing just one more.

Our lives consist, it seems, of endless entreaties for "just one more." As a kid, I would cajole my father to read to me just one more story (shameful confession – from a comic book!) before I had to put the light out and go to sleep. Forty-odd years ago, when he was in his 40s, UU Pete Seeger wrote in a column that he was a "cheeseophile." Come what might, he said, he would always yearn for "one more bite of cheese, one more song ... one more kiss." At one of his Sunday morning discussions, Edwin Benton posed the question "what keeps you going?" "One more" was the common thread woven through the group's sundry responses: to put one more child through school, to see the outcome of one more election ...

To flatter ourselves that there will always be time for just *one* more, is our attempt to bargain with our own mortality, to smudge the hard-edged fact that *some* time *will* be The Last. The venerable author/interlocutor Studs Terkel said he always thought ninety would be an acceptable length in years for a good life. Now that he is ninety-two, he says, "Well, you know, ninety-three would be nice." A condemned prisoner's last meal, though it fulfill every Lucullan culinary wish, must be a joyless affair, for weighing close and heavy over the convict's plate is the knowledge that there will never, *ever* be another meal.

The last "For What It's Worth?" Actually, I have yet to fob off on this page one or two pieces already written. By then, maybe I'll notice something I overlooked in my seemingly bare closet of ideas. Well, you know, just one more would be nice...

# DON'T BE TOO SURE

Years ago, and backed into a scholastic corner, I finally set my jaw and elected the Physics 101 course I'd skirted in dread for years. Amidst all the daunting equations, however, I do remember the pleasure I took in learning about Heisenberg's uncertainty principle, wherein that German scientist held that the very act of *observing* the behavior of subatomic particles altered the behavior of said particles. The implication was you couldn't be sure of anything, even what was right in front of your own eyes. Ever since then, I've morphed the uncertainty principle into my own life style of principled uncertainty.

Other hard science courses taught me that much of what we now accept as Reality (should that be in quotes?) actually may or may not be correct or true. The theory (dictionary-defined as "assumption, speculation, supposition") of such things as continental drift, evolution, even the Big Bang that brought all Creation into being, are essentially our best educated guesses about reality. They are place holders until a better explanation comes along, just as better explanations superseded earlier "scientific facts" that the Earth is the center of the universe and is also flat. I cherish the story of how Albert Einstein was once buttonholed by some other eminent physicist who, for 20 minutes, pointed out all the "mistakes" in Einstein's Theory of Relativity. Einstein listened patiently, then with flat objectivity replied, "That's what you think."

In the less tangible disciplines such as philosophy, theology and politics, truth gets slipperier still - and more dangerous. Indeed, cocksureness may be seen as a roadblock to freedom and democracy. On retiring after fifty years of writing political commentary, New York Times columnist Anthony Lewis said one great lesson he'd learned is that "certainty is the enemy of decency and humanity in people who are sure they are right, like Osama bin Laden and John Ashcroft." Judge Learned Hand described our nation's political foundation this way: "The spirit of liberty is the spirit that is not too sure it is right." And Unitarian Oliver Wendell Holmes said absolute truth is elusive and that there are a range of plausible views in a democracy. Despots, naturally, can't abide this. Did Hitler sponsor lots of public forums so the people could discuss the veracity of his policies and beliefs?

Spiritually, thousands have never rallied 'neath Uncertainty's banner. Rather, most people have flocked to this or that prophet, all of whom claimed to reveal the one and only True Word of God. Only trouble is, as musician Mark Knopfler once wrote in a song verse about soapbox orators, "Two men say they're Jesus; *one* of them must be wrong." We UUs have built our paradoxical doubting faith on the premise that all the world's religions contain part of, but not the entire Truth. We reserve the freedom and the right to select what seems true to our own hearts and to leave the rest, as well as to modify our selections as we gain new insights. In our weekly services and free discussions, we regularly reenact the blind ones describing their touched part of the elephant of Truth. And it's a lifelong endeavor because, while Truth may be large as an elephant, it's of a substance more resembling mercury than granite.

# HURRY UP AND ...

Watched a TV show last night. Darndest thing. On network, not public, TV. No doctors, lawyers or cops; no explosions, car chases or shoot-outs (many commercials, though); no rude language (unless the word "death" offends you). All about pace of life speeding up in our society, everything must be faster, *faster*! Decided to try keeping up by eliminating words – articles, conjunctions, nouns – from sentences, thereby saving one or two seconds ("important!" those interviewed said) of writing / reading. But realized, by stopping to explain that, thus gave up the few seconds gained. Besides, was sounding less like Richard, more like a robot. Anyhow, this show hooked me by acknowledging they wouldn't provide all the answers, "...but, boy, have we got questions!" I was just reading in my "Story of Philosophy" library book how some guy named Socrates used the same ploy about 2,500 years ago. In fact, at SUUS, we still do this each week after coffee; we call it "discussion." Far out, huh?

The program traced our current "faster!" fixation to the advent of the touch-tone telephone. Nowadays even I, descended from sloths, not ocelots, find the rare rotary-dial I encounter an irritating dawdle. But, it seems, technological "advances" eventually change us not only psychologically but physiologically too, altering our very brain cell biology. Pedestrians interviewed said when calling friends (on their cell phones, of course), they hung up impatiently after the *third* unanswered ring. Teens complained that three, even *two*, seconds of silence (now *there's* a rude word!) between CD song tracks was "way long." And almost anything less than instantaneous is no longer fast enough for fast food. Eating food? Why, nobody *just* eats anymore. You must eat *while* doing something else – like driving a car.

11

Things got positively spiritual when the show attributed this accelerating frenzy to the baby boomers' realization that they, too, *are* eventually going to die. Their response has been, "cram more in, speed life up!" But wait! Does this make sense? If you're approaching a place where you'd just as soon not arrive, do you start to *run* toward it? Wouldn't you sooner drop down and start to crawl by inches? Does anyone still take time to smell the roses, to be in the moment?

According to the program's talking heads, some do, many don't. They divide our society into two types. Some are of a reflective, contemplative nature, less enamored of the multi-processing, fast-track life. Some of the more analytical of this type wind up at UU church doors; some even stay for discussion. For many others, however, the *unexamined* life is the only kind worth living. To avoid uncomfortable self-appraisal, they rely heavily on external stimuli, provided most often these days by the TV remote and the computer mouse. For this type, a week at Thoreau's Walden cabin holds about as much appeal as a stretch in solitary at Sing Sing.

In one way, at least, these hyperactive boomers have successfully retreated from advancing age: their average attention span has regressed to that of a three year-old. And maybe those brain chemistry changes wrought by technology are seeping through all of society. Some AT&T sales rep. interviewed said a real growth market currently is Lancaster County, Penn., where every month she sells more and more cell phones ...to the Amish.

# THE DUCK

Driving to my new job, I pass a very small pond which last fall attracted its share of migrating ducks. Clusters of two, three, four ducks spotted various parts of the water, but I noticed that one in particular kept to itself at the pond's end nearest the road. I started to romanticize, anthropomorphize this bird shamelessly. This solitary, quiescent, contemplative creature became a Zen duck, a Thoreau duck – it was *my* duck.

November's chill became December's cold freeze. Ice began to spread over the pond. Some few ducks bobbed in spots of still-open water, but my duck floated surrounded by ice. Was this just wafer-thin skim ice? Was the bird stuck?

Sensing the interconnectedness of this Earthly web of life, I began to think about the duck more frequently. At night and in the morning, I dwelt on its uncertain predicament and fate. And in my concern and pathos I learned two things: I am surprisingly – and rather appallingly – ignorant of the mechanics of Nature, and the weave of this interconnected web of which we are a part is a lot more complex than I realized.

Each day I drove by, there was the duck in the same place in the ice. I surmised that the bird must be imprisoned and that without intervention, it would eventually die. Once or twice, I saw some other duck nearby – was it the same duck, perhaps its mate? Maybe this "mate" was feeding its companion – do ducks do that? Is altruism wired into duck genes or is it every mallard for itself?

Well, maybe *I* should try to feed the duck. Uh...feed it what? I remembered tossing torn bread to the ducks when I was a kid, but is that really good for ducks? What if that was like trying to sustain a starving person with Krispy Kremes and Cap'n Crunch? Would insects be better? Frogs? Salamanders? What *do* ducks eat anyway? I thought further. If I approached the duck to feed it, shouldn't I just try to chop it out of the ice in the first place? But then the bird might panic, thrash around and injure itself or even go into cardiac arrest and die. Do ducks *have* heart attacks?

Besides, I recalled a years-old news story of two naturalists who were censured for trying to rescue a deer stuck in similar circumstances. The countervailing opinion was that environmentalists should observe but not interject themselves to alter the course of Nature's events. And during each day I pitied my one lone duck, how many thousand others were killed by hunters and predators? Uh...do ducks have predators?

My drive to work became a death watch. Each day I waited to see the duck's limp head collapsed on the ice in death. But each day the head remained upright on its arched neck. How long does it take a duck ...to ...starve?

December proved mild and pools of melted ice appeared around my duck. Perhaps Nature would free its own prisoner. Overnight rain after Christmas caused some ice to heave, and I passed to see my duck listing 45 degrees. The angle revealed to me not webbed duck feet but the square wooden base ... of a carved, painted decoy.

Immediately, I saw myself as the forehead-slap, complete fool. I berated myself for pouring out all my sorrow and pity onto a phony duck. But I recalled Robert Frost who, after first wanting to shush an annoying bird, later decided "there must be something wrong in wanting to silence any song." Likewise, I concluded that empathy and compassion can only come from good places in the human soul and thus cannot be wrong – even if directed toward a block of wood.

## AM I BORING YOU?

Ow! Just a flesh wound, but it drew some blood. The injuring instrument was "Books Make You a Boring Person," a column I read in (all together now) the Sunday Times book section. It contended that some people use a text the way others use Muzak: to stave off any silence of their own minds. They fortify every domestic locale – the night table, the dining counter, the *bathroom*, even their own pockets – with reading matter, lest they ever have an empty moment. But their pursuit is sycophantic; their reading is an intellectual crutch. We all know people, the author argued, who have read everything but have nothing of their own to say.

Well, yes. In fact, touché – up to a point. Once again, I felt embarrassingly exposed by a writer who never even met me. I had to acknowledge that my nose is intermittently in things I'm reading from the time I sit at the breakfast table to the time I recline on my pillow at bedtime. I even confess to stuffing unfinished articles in my back pocket to fill unanticipated free moments during the day. I do *not*, however, stock the bathroom in advance – I, uh, just grab whatever periodical is closest when I answer the call.

And when I was 20, I, too, started with a genuflecting stance toward books and the opinions expressed in them. Indeed, I was fully one of Emerson's "meek young men grow[ing] up in libraries, believing it their duty to accept the views which Cicero, which Locke, which Bacon have given". It took me many years to be able to appropriate unto myself the part that followed Emerson's semicolon: "forgetful that Cicero, Locke and Bacon were only young men in libraries when they wrote those books."

My own doubt seed germinated from a long-ago (1960s) Russell Baker column that advocated the audacious notion that book burning might not always be an act of unmitigated evil. We routinely recycle – burn – newspapers and magazines containing all manner of writers' ideas and opinions, ranging from claptrap to holy writ, *but*, Baker said, just let any village dolt get his printed ravings sandwiched between two cardboard covers and suddenly this is a sacred object, the burning of which is a cardinal intellectual sin.

At this, Thoreau's different drummer began beating a tattoo in my mind. Don't forget, I reasoned, that "Mein Kampf" first infected the world as – a book. And hadn't I myself first sat in a Unitarian church because I couldn't accept the views of no less than Christendom's holiest book, the Bible? So I began my lifelong jousting with books, august and obscure. Now I even don't finish books that haven't won me over by the time I'm half through them. It's said some books should be tasted, some chewed and only a select few completely swallowed and digested.

In fact, I regard myself as some mental cow, a ruminant consuming bales of idea fodder, to later regurgit ... uh, make that reconfigure it in new, synthesized form. Nothing to say? Ask anyone who has sat, eyeballs glazing over, through a Sunday talkback with me.

I was gratified the "...Boring Person" author and I wound up in agreement. She concluded, "We do better to wrestle our writers as Jacob with the angel than to worship them as saviors." I can feel my flesh wound healing nicely; I don't think there'll be a scar.

# A SOAPBOX FOR HENRY

In this sesquicentennial (don't grab the dictionary – it's 150th) year of Thoreau's "Walden," I thought I might again step behind one of my preferred polemical podiums. Let's see, this one's been pushed aside of late. I'll just dust it off a bit – there...

Moderately long ago, circa 1960, UU Ray Bradbury wrote a poetic/ominous fantasy story about a singular sight he witnessed in suburban Los Angeles. Guided by her husband, a woman walked her dog while listening to a portable radio through a tiny earphone plugged in her ear. Bradbury watched, stunned, as the somnambulist, transported to and enchanted by myriad distant aural worlds, was helped up and down curbs by a man who otherwise might as well not have been there at all.

Now, over 40 years into 1960's future, I read an article about people talking on cell phones while walking (never even mind about driving!) who are colliding obliviously into other pedestrians and stepping without heed into street traffic, some of them to their deaths.

To me, these two stories are linked on a spiritual plain by a sermon comment by UU minister Forrest Church, defining sin as "anything that divides us: within ourselves; against our neighbor; from the ground of our being." By this measure, we are fast – and happily! – turning this techno society into one vast swamp of iniquity.

This was evident even in the dim, dusky corners of history – what, five, seven years ago? – when the Internet was new and cable news was replete with stories of divorces – humans rent apart – due to spouses locking themselves in rooms to spend literal days at a time on the

Web. More recently, I phoned a New Haven nightclub to inquire about concert tickets. After long minutes spent listening to ninety-three pre-recorded menu options, none of which would answer my questions, I reached a human receptionist who was audibly irritated that I had breached her computer-generated Maginot Line. She stopped just short of scolding me for talking with her. Well, I wondered, what else does she, a telephone operator, get paid to do all day?

Science fiction/fantasy writers have a disconcerting habit of being more predictive than speculative. H. G. Wells acidly said his epitaph should read, "G-dd-mn you all, I told you so." We cringe and shudder at movies depicting future worlds where humans have become as emotionless as the machines that run their societies. Yet we are like proverbial frogs in a pot of gradually boiling water, contentedly unaware they're on their way to becoming frogs' legs with garlic. Our open arms embrace every techno innovation, inconsiderate that each one may slice off another sliver of our souls.

We (should, if we don't) marvel that when we need computer advice, we can pull a machine from our back pockets and talk to a person (actually not called a person, but "tech support") in Jaipur, India. Imagine – we push several buttons and converse with someone living on the opposite side of Earth. And do we inquire about their weather, their food, their cities, their beliefs? No, our only interest in them is that they tell us what key to press on our gizmo. I never thought of Thoreau as a science-fiction writer, but one hundred and fifty years ago, in "Walden," he noted a new telegraph line linking Maine and Texas and commented, "but Maine and Texas, it may be, have nothing important to communicate."

# PILGRIM'S PLUMBING PROGRESS

My toilet broke. It refused to stop running even after the tank refilled. My trusted – and only known – remedy of jiggling the handle was impotent to affect it. My Plan B was always "call the plumber," but the stock market's recent tanking (no pun intended) had rendered this option fiscally profligate. I was forced to resort to the dreaded Plan C: do-it-yourself repair.

Plumbing happens. But for me, who has to remember which way the light bulb unscrews to change it, this secular nuisance was a predicament of truly metaphysical proportions. Job on the ash heap was no more beset by tribulations. In fact, this only confirmed for me my lately espoused view that it's a cold, Godless Universe we inhabit. Even the cruelest God would not condemn me to the ninth circle of Hell for the mechanically disinclined. Well, I consoled myself, if I undertook this myself and got in over my head, so to speak, I could always call the plumber to bail me out – uh, so to speak. So, recalling my last mutual fund financial statement, I girded my loins and broke into the old spiritual, "You got to cross that lonesome valley by yourself."

I went to the library and chose two plumbing repair books with schematic diagrams and big color pictures. These would be my Virgils. I didn't see any of those "…for Idiots" volumes on plumbing. Scrupulously following these manuals, I determined – my best guess – which parts were kaput and hadda go. At the hardware store, I bought replacement pieces for about $10, so at this point I figured I was a good hundred and fifty bucks ahead of the game.

But my path was not unstoned. A vital piece of flexible pipe to connect the tank to the water shutoff valve, guaranteed to fit all sizes, didn't, of course. The mighty waters issued forth from both ends of the fitting. My God, my God, why hast Thou forsaken me? Oh, yeah – forgot. Ain't no such. I returned the part to the hardware store, where a real, live Virgil – whose monogrammed store shirt said "Alan" – informed me that the adapter ring I needed was in part of the packaging I hadn't yet unwrapped. Oh.

Came the hour, after much grunting, cursing and twisting, when my time of utilitarian judgment was at hand. My repairs were complete and I was ready to refill the tank, then flush. My lips a thin line, I inched the water shutoff valve back open. Water hissed and gurgled and gradually filled the tank – and my connecting pipe stayed dry as the Sinai! Now the flush. The water whooshed away, then swished back in. It crept back up in the tank to the "fill level". . . and stopped! Jubilate and hosanna! My elation was no less than that of the NASA engineers after Neil Armstrong stepped off the lunar module. I tried to resist a gloating image of me, adjustable wrench in hand, with my foot up on the recumbent toilet tank Goliath. Maybe God *was* in Heaven and all was right after all.

For several days thereafter, using the facilities "chez moi" was more than just attending to a body function; it was a testament to my triumph. But then, driving to work one morning, I heard strange noises when I applied the brakes. "Oh, please no. Father, if Thou be willing, take away this cup from me…"

# IN BETWEEN SYSTEMS

I (nor you, either, tolerant reader) never know what will set me off. After breakfast, I brush my teeth while listening to the TV weather report from the set around the corner, in the bedroom. The chirpy forecaster, describing the upcoming blue-sky day surrounded by rainstorms yesterday and tomorrow, said, "We're in between systems." This phrase stuck. Through a mouthful of wintergreen foam, I sputtered, "Hah! In life, aren't we, all of us, *always* in between systems?" We may see happiness, joy as what brightens our life/sky in between clouds of disappointment, sorrow, even routine boredom. Granted this, I found it no large step at all from Dr. Don, the weather guy, to Leo Tolstoy, a quote from whom I came upon the same day: "There is no happiness in life, only occasional flares of it. You must learn to live on them."

On first visiting the home of my former partner, Nancy, I noticed three wall plaques embellished with jig-sawed wooden butterflies. Together they spelled out the phrase, "Catch joy as it flies by." Nineteen years later, I will own that my initial (unspoken) reaction was, "pret-ty hokey." Life in the interim has humbled me, allowing me to see a certain profundity I missed in my first smug reading. For joy, like Emily Dickinson's hope, is, indeed, a thing with feathers that flies free, frustrating our efforts to control it on a leash. My continual attempts to drive joy into a corner and make it bow to my will have been repeatedly rebuffed. *Rats! That wasn't as much fun as I'd so carefully planned for.* Whereas, other times joy, like the unexpected sighting of a rare and beautiful bird, has come upon me by surprise, thus taking my spiritual breath away all the more notably.

This "joy bird" visited me literally last summer. As I pulled my car out onto (sparsely traversed, fortunately) Middle Road, a fat-breasted robin swooped down and paced the car three feet from my windshield for an entire block. It was wondrously surreal, a life-imitating-special effects scene, and joy – certainly not *I* – was steering the Toyota down *that* block. And I still recall 30 years ago, gassing up at a Mobil station. The mechanic and I gaped as two mallard ducks strolled nonchalantly across the asphalt 10 feet away from us. Normally a stone-faced Yankee, this mechanic blurted, "Boy, something like that'll make your whole day!"

This is not to say only aviary encounters count. Joy can flutter in as a sound, a taste, a touch … a memory. Obviously, it's not only winning the $10 million lottery. Benjamin Franklin said, "Human felicity is produced not so much by great pieces of good fortune that seldom happen as by little advantages that occur every day."

Tolstoy says we must sustain ourselves on life's occasional flares of happiness. It seems joy is to us what a fat and protein-rich feast was to our early ancestors. Since the first humans never knew when the next mastodon meal might come ambling along, they adapted to storing fat in their cells for the famine times in between. Just so, we should store up happiness as sweet whipped cream to sustain our souls. "Catch joy as it flies by." It comes in between systems.

# ELUSIVE BONBON

At one of Edwin Benton's fledgling Sunday morning discussions (may they sprout strong wings and soar!) the topic was that elusive bonbon, happiness. The participants exchanged much wisdom – wish I could remember what it was. But the conversation stirred up enough of my thoughts on happiness for me to pour out the scramble as this column.

We all want it. We already have some of it. Many (most?) crave more of it. But studies (by "experts," be warned) indicate limits for our yearnings. Research postulates happiness "set points," inborn, pre-set happiness levels, to which we always return despite temporary spikes up or down. Hit big in the lottery and your giddiness will simmer down to your former regular level; receive a dire diagnosis and your gloom will eventually buoy back up to your innate happiness set point.

A five-minute chat with anybody will reveal that, like similarly postulated body weight set points, these levels are different for each of us. This begs the question we UUs often ask regarding other precious commodities: on a scale from mild contentment to mind-reeling jubilation, how much happiness is reasonably "enough" for us to possess in good conscience?

Differing views of just what the "desirable" level of happiness is are probably as old as the divergent cults of Apollo vs. Dionysus in Ancient Greece. As a denomination, UUs have pitched their tent in the Apollonian camp of reason and rationality, leaving more fervid, Dionysian exultations of faith – twirling, arm-waving, gospel-shouting, tongue-speaking exuberances – to evangelicals of all persuasions. Our emotionally tepid belief that religion should *make sense*, thought odd by multitudes, has given rise to quips that "UUs are God's frozen people" and "a UU service is a book review, a clarinet solo, then a discussion."

Granted, our ruminative nature may well tamp down exuberant spirits. During a Sunday morning concert service, folksinger Charlie King told us there never was a happy occasion that he couldn't ruin by thinking it to death. But when we consider the reality of this world, of which our religion is an inseparable part, it's hard to be too happy about how it's all going. We also await further evidence that happiness is guaranteed us in some heaven afterwards. Writer Jon Krakauer said believers are happy but happiness isn't as important as being free to think for yourself. Further, our restraint guards against spilling into the intolerant fanaticism that mars major world religions. Joyce Carol Oates said enthusiasm's darker face is invariably impatience with those who decline to share its predilections.

Lest I come off too much the sour New England apple, let me here confess my own recent dalliance with hedonistic happiness. Before church, my Sunday mornings consist of one eye on the clock, my Prufrock-measured breakfast and the measured strains of NPR's "Sunday Baroque." Very serene, very...dull. Suddenly impatient, I switched the radio to my new tape of barrelhouse blues slide guitar. My knees bounced to the raunchy rasp of those boogie-woogie strings, and next thing I knew, I (even I!) was dancing – albeit stiffly – around the living room. Oops! Clock indicated I was five minutes behind schedule. So what?! At song's end I was big-grin happy. I don't think I'd like to check my brain at the gates of ecstasy in order to live there, but now and then it's sure a rockin' place to visit.

26

# MEMORIAL GARDEN, CHRISTMAS MORNING

By temperament, I am no hale-fellow, well met, a boisterous type who closes the place (though, ironically, in the latest gun-notch on my checkered job history, I am required to help close the grocery store where I lately toil). Rather, I am a solitary, first-up early riser, the type who opens places. So it was that I arrived at SUUS on Christmas Sunday morning, the first of 17 souls to gather in our meeting room on that far-flung day.

With no other cars to jockey among, I pulled up directly in line with our memorial garden. Feeling no urgency to jump out, get inside and start things going, I indulged in some solemn minutes observing this hallowed place. I reflected on how well our burial ground articulates to me beliefs that help form my faith. For me, (I dare speak for no one else), the overarching presumption of this faith is that we humans, for all our technologies, for all our sacred fable/myth stories and legends, we humans are not separate from (let alone "above") the rest of natural Creation. In (my) truth, we are but one more puzzle piece of the whole Universe. As one of our (proselytizing?) pamphlets says, there is no conflict between religion and the world, the sacred and the secular, since they all have their source in the same reality.

Our cemetery manifests to me this essential unity with the natural world. Indeed, save for a wrought iron bench and a bronze plaque (itself affixed to an unsculpted boulder) noting those who repose there, one might take this space for any graceful path in the woods. The memorial garden is simply a stone walkway and a rock wall framed by bushes and trees. Flowers bloom there in season.

 There are no tombstones and certainly none of the gravesite sculptures that, to my eye, range from curios to grotesqueries. Below the ground, no teak and cement coffins protect corporeal remains from the "ravages" of time. Instead, our dead have already been transformed to ashes, willingly to facilitate their ultimate reunion with the Earth, whence all life came.

What human elements there are in the garden are not at odds with the Earth but rather endeavor to be part of it. The pathway is not of asphalt or cement, but of squared stones. Builders of old erected huge pyramids and soaring cathedrals to transcend – abandon – the Earth and reach to a Heaven. Our wall is of roughhewn stone and low, as if to hug the Earth, our home. What soaring there is is done by the massive-trunked pines, symbols of steadfastness, perpetuity, eternity itself.

Finally I addressed what to me was initially a grating note in the garden's composition: the close proximity of the church school's playground equipment (thankfully not of garish-hued plastic). I used to feel that the kids' energetic cries and yells intruded on the garden's solemnity, but I came to see this overlap as a reminder that death is not separate from but an inextricable part of life, and that in the midst of life, we encounter death. Conversely, children, like the garden's flowers, are proof that, despite death, life always renews itself.

Another car pulled into the parking lot. I got out of my car and walked to greet Helen and her daughter Margaret. We went into the church, soon to begin what would be for me the second religious service of this Christmas morning.

# FROST ON THE ECONOMY

I've recorded my thoughts (filled space) here before about the slippery, elusive nature of "reality", whatever that may be, what with blind men and elephants and glasses half empty or full. So I was surprised once when someone said this column provided them with wisdom each month. …Wisdom? Me? Are you talkin' to me?!

Strange – I'd always thought this page was my public therapist's couch where, like therapists (and, so I've read, ministers too), I wrestled with, and maybe even worked through, my own life's angst and anxieties. If this produced any wisdom as an incidental by-product, well, gravy.

All this is a rambling preface to just one small insight offered this time, a thought from Robert Frost I encountered recently: "Well spent is synonymous with kept." I found in this graceful line a persuasive idea, one that sent a ripple of re-evaluation through my anal-retentive (therapists' jargon) mind. My mind remains that of the little boy who took to heart perhaps too well that fable about the ant and the grasshopper. My goal of saving for tomorrow overrides living for today.

Since I wasn't on a drop-by-for-coffee footing with ol' Robert, I can't say with authority, but my guess is Frost wasn't talking about necessities. We all have to pay the electric bill and buy milk. I think he was referring to life's embellishments, and Plato said it's not in life's necessities but in it's luxuries that we count ourselves rich – enriched. Heck, inmates in Levenworth have meals, clothes and a roof over their heads, but I wouldn't cite them as role models for lives of enrichment.

So after necessities plus prudent allocations for savings and charity (all homely blessings to be grateful for), what are we to do with what monies we have left? If it is not "well-spent" on *something*, what about the money itself if kept? I get no intrinsic pleasure from the stuff. Unlike Disney's Scrooge McDuck, I am not thrilled (nor have I enough of it) to "burrow through it like a gopher and toss it up and let it hit me on the head." Shall I sit with my money in a room and watch a clock tick till the hour hand tolls the time when I will die? And upon that hour to die, will I, in Thoreau's phrase, realize I have not lived? What is a life if not our experiences throughout it? At our lives' end, what are we but the sum of all our memories of our experiences? What we choose (to the extent that we can) these experiences to be will make our lives either rich or barren.

Thus I bought myself a CD of some favorite music, without which, Frank Zappa said, life is "just a bunch of boring production deadlines and dates by which bills must be paid." Then I went to see a Japanese anime movie whose surreal, swirling images will forever color the palate of my memories. And I remembered a poem that counsels if all your worldly goods are reduced to two loaves of bread, sell one loaf to buy some hyacinths for your soul. Sound advice, I thought – just don't tell Aesop's industrious ant.

# THANKS: MY THREE

On the Sunday after Thanksgiving, I structured our morning service around the premise of having various members describe three things in their personal lives for which they were grateful. The following is a somewhat extended (shamelessly padded?) description of my chosen three. Apologies for any disabling déja vu suffered by those who were in attendance.

In the past six years of living alone, I've come to see myself as sort of a male Emily Dickinson – behaviorally, that is; most certainly *not* linguistically. I too have had a lover's quarrel with the world (which I perhaps instigated). To resolve this argument, I have more and more avoided the other party – that is, the world. Thus, I've become quite the hermit. However, certain connections to the estranged world remain important – vital – to me, and I am grateful for the following three: the window, public broadcasting and SUUS – you.

When my former partner, Nancy, moved in with me, she needed room for her many house plants, so we had installed the dining room greenhouse window. Today the window remains just past my breakfast table, a roughly 7 x 4 foot expanse of three convex glass panels.

At dawn and dusk, when my spiritual awareness is most acute, the window showcases for me my yard's trees and the background sky – the natural Earth on which I'm living. During my sacrosanct morning meal, I watch trunks and leaves emerge from night black, first as silhouettes, later as sunlit colors of the season. I witness the year cycle from bare branch to red bud, through green leaf back again to red and yellow parchment.

In late afternoon, the window occasionally frames postcard-dramatic sunsets, for the duration of which I simply stand there and stare. I also behold Earth's sporadic tantrums – windswept torrents and piling blizzards, orchestrated to howling, splattering and crashing. Impressed, enthralled, even intimidated, I remain always the grateful viewer.

Though some would dismiss "relationships" with radio and TV personalities as poor substitute for real human flesh and bone, I have come to appreciate the limited interaction with my mealtimes PBS company. I share breakfast with Morning Edition's Steve Inskeep and Renee Montaigne (I confess I actually *miss* avuncular Bob Edwards) and I have dinner with the News Hour's tad-fuddy Jim Lehrer. Unfailingly pleasant, no matter what my own mood, they inform me daily on events in my eschewed world. Moreover, they provide me with much source material for the quirky anecdotes which, as Ringo once said, "loom large in my legend." And I don't have to make myself presentable – or even decent – to welcome them in.

But most thanks I give for SUUS members, my unofficial "aunts, uncles and cousins" with whom I have a family "reunion" each Sunday (even Emily Dickinson had family). I do realize SUUS's limits. In a way, I'm attending a weekly stockholders' meeting of a limited liability corporation. I'm not obligated to return home with any member to raise children, pay bills or take out the garbage. But for a few Sunday hours, this outsider knows he'll feel welcome in this enclave of guileless question-askers. I feel comfortable knowing that members will disregard my tics and warts and will instead remind me of better aspects of my nature. Nor am I singled out for special handling; at SUUS this is SOP.

So, though I have partly secluded myself from the world, my perhaps peculiar connections – Nature, the march of human events and my faith family – sustain me.

For these, many thanks.

# WHAT I MEAN TO SAY IS …

Over the recent year's end holidays, our minister, Kim, reminded us of the sometimes hidden meaning of gifts, the unspoken message(s) the giver can send to the recipient along with the material object itself. Later in that service, I shared a memory of customized Christmas cards my artist father drew for me when I was a teenager. I went home and excavated the cards from their closet storage and lo! After forty years, I saw again the hidden message Dad sent me in between the lines "Merry Christmas, Rich."

In fact, we don't even have to be trying for our words or deeds to be (mis)taken for other than what they are. Before Christmas, I slowed my car to a stop in front of a house to admire its beautiful door decoration. I warmly imagined a couple inside seeing me: "Oh, look George! That man outside appreciates our heirloom wreath." Then the reverie darkened; what if they see me as a burglar casing their joint before the heist?

It astonishes me how much time and effort we human beings expend on trying to understand just exactly what it is that other humans are saying to us. It ain't easy. Recently, I saw the 1935 film, "Mutiny On the Bounty," where Franchot Tone delivered my favorite line. As an HMS Bounty officer ashore in Tahiti, where he's compiling a dictionary of the inhabitants' language, he declares admiringly to the island's chief, "Your language is most un-English. It says exactly what it means." Conversely, I recall a later film, "Cool Hand Luke," where one character's take on every snafu the plot presented was, "What we've got here is a failure to communicate."

Doctors from Freud ("Freudian slip") to Eric ("Games People Play") Berne have elaborated the ways

37

people say other than what they mean. In fact, a stock joke in that field has two psychiatrists passing in the hospital hallway. One says, "Good morning," and the other thinks, "Hmmm, I wonder what he meant by that." Psychologist Deborah Tannen built her career writing books about the language gap that constitutes the "no man's (sic) land" between men and women in the gender wars. And don't look for peace to flower soon; her first bore the pessimistic title, "You Just Don't Understand."

The wicket gets stickier still because with linguistic devices such as irony, the *whole idea* is to say other than what you mean. We wake up to wind-driven sleet and mutter, "*Lovely* morning!" Of course, you must judge well which words are ironic and which earnest. Some people *like* sleet. Space precludes my pontificating about deconstruction literary analysis or the Byzantine indirection of international diplomatic language, but you begin to see the ubiquity of communication obfuscation – is that, uh, clear?

All this leads me to ask, in all cynical wonderment, how, then, it can be that untold millions of people, from desert terrorist schools to drive-in megachurches in middle America, seem to understand each other perfectly when they use a certain three-letter word, namely G-O-D. They have absolutely no doubt what this word means, whereas I have heard God described as a bearded grandfather, a principle – or particle – of physics or "a large invertebrate." Maybe Orthodox Jews have the right idea to proscribe writing or speaking the word altogether. But then I heard an end-run around this dictum which cited God as "the unnameable namer."

…The merry-go-round spins on.

# PICKERS, CHOOSERS, PRUNERS, BUILDERS

Among the many, *many* things (don't get me started) that cause my oh so judgmental nose to crinkle in disdain are condensed books and network broadcasts of films "edited for content." I don't want anyone else deciding for me what to eliminate from some entire work in order to maintain my interest – let alone to "protect me" morally, politically or spiritually. But recently I looked anew around my own living room, at things I surround myself with that are meaningful to me, and I realized my "get-thee-behind-me-editor" stance did rather resemble Janus' face – or two faces.

For instance, I have a recording of Handel's complete "Messiah" – naturally, wrong-century Rich has it on four vinyl LP records. And I once experienced the entire oratorio at Carnegie Hall; the performance lasted almost five hours. But most Christmases and Easters, my ears and spirit float equally high on my single LP of Bernstein/ N.Y. Philharmonic "Messiah" highlights. While I do own a boxed set of Shakespeare's complete plays, I cherish – and will turn to more often – my recent purchase of "Speak the Speech: the Shakespeare Quotation Book," wherein the Bard's lines of most eternal resonance are compiled for ready reference. *Several* Holy Bibles actually sit on my bookshelves. I've read the synoptic Gospels and sundry Old Testament books, but I readily admit I've never plowed from first page to last through the entire Christians' Scripture.

Occasionally, I do my homework. Before Mark Schenker's Sunday service on same, I reread Emerson's "Self-Reliance." I appreciate it more each time (a definition of "classic"?), but I also acknowledged that Emerson is, for me, a bit of a tough cerebral slog. For comparison, I glanced over an edited version of the essay and the editor's stated purpose came as a light-bulb revelation to me: "I came to think of the essays as gardens in which [my] underlined passages were magnificent flowers – and all the rest a rampant and choking growth of nineteenth-century rhetorical weeds and vines that were best… cut back." He felt that an abridged version could make Emerson's wisdom more accessible to those deterred by his sometimes long, difficult passages.

I realized an editor didn't have to be a condenser/censor – he or she could also be a pruner, an assembler. Moreover, I saw that this very process is what has built up our modern U.U. spiritual amalgam. In drawing from the wisdom of all the world's religions, we have selected, pruned – edited – from their cultural and temporal weed growths, those parts which remain true and meaningful for us here and now. Our forebear, Thomas Jefferson, epitomized this with his "Jefferson Bible," in which he literally edited the New Testament to extract only those teachings of Jesus that harmonized with his own ideals (and if it comes to letting someone else decide what words to eliminate, I'd sooner trust Thomas Jefferson than John Ashcroft).

Finally, I saw that I myself, with a self-reliance to make Ralph Waldo proud, have worked for decades in this tradition to produce my very own venerated text ("The Wisdom of the Ages: the Gressley Condensation"?): a dog-eared manila file folder laconically labeled "Quotes." It contains my unique collection of lines and passages which, since the sixties, I've culled from various texts – the Bhagavad Gita to the N.Y. Times – and figures – Lao-Tse to anonymous blues singers. From all these, I've custom-built the spiritual edifice in which I try to live my life. I resist the temptation to say, "It has made me what I am today" – much too easy for that to be a punch line.

# COLD TURKEY MOMENT

After nine years of cohabitation, living alone offered (if little else) the chance to custom design how I filled my days. So now, in my increasingly-late middle age, and with quasi-Buddhist focus on Intent, I decided to devote as many of my off-work solo hours as possible to what gratified me most. And this most-rewarding activity (aside from food preparation/consumption, an explanation of which would require a book, not a column) came down to be what I'll call information gathering.

My life seems to be one endless quest to accumulate more facts, figures and viewpoints in order to better live said life. I've bought the idea that the more I know about what's going on both in the world around me and also (God help us) inside my own head, the more comfortable with my life I'll become.

I pursue this end along two avenues of media: print and $20^{th}$- century electronic, by which I mean radio and television – no computers. Ever since a guest speaker (salesman?) from the New York Times convinced my ninth grade history class (well, this student anyway) of the virtues of daily newspaper reading, I've been a Times junkie. This is supplemented with a list of library books – mainly psychology/sociology, never fiction (save for the occasional re-reading of my cherished "Moby Dick," a source of insights as deep as the ocean depths its sacred text evokes). On TV, not for me the latest "Survivor" or "American Idol". Rather, it was PBS, CNN, C-Span – leavened only by some barbeque or ice cream show on the Food Channel ... the pattern emerges. Now in our digitized, miniaturized, computerized new century, maybe we're all a bit information-manic. But with my obsessive leanings, I realized my lifestyle "choice" was becoming a lifestyle addiction. My presence for "All Things Considered" was no longer a pleasant preference; it was a tyrannical compulsion. And, habitually early for work, I *had* to fill those five minutes I would sit in the car by reading one last page of my current book.

The extremity of my condition became clear one morning when, halfway to work, I discovered I had left my book home! My discomfiture edged close to panic; I fought the visceral urge to return home for it. After I parked in my accustomed space, I staved off DT's by rereading a book review torn from Sunday's paper that lay on the passenger's seat. That finished, I gazed out the car window and, by surprise, was completely engaged in reverie.

I saw six seagulls perched at the very apex of a gable on the nearby Wal-Mart. First I marveled at their winged otherness and at the insouciance of their repose on what was, to me, a dizzying height. Next, the birds became emblems of this New England shoreline, beloved locus of halcyon childhood vacations spent in summer seaside cabins, and where today I am fortunate (blessed?) to reside. Then I recalled my late artist father. Dad would punctuate his seascapes with gulls in painter shorthand. A resting seagull was an upward-turned white crescent on a black brushstroke of legs; a flying gull was simply a white V in his sky.

Time to punch in. With renewed sense of place and legacy, I got out of the car. For those media-deprived minutes I might have been less well-informed about my world, but with each step I took, I felt more firmly grounded on this Earth on which I was living.

44

# LIVING AS ART

File this, I suppose, under Top 10 Golden Clichés, right up there with "count your blessings" and "life is what you make it." Interestingly though, most golden clichés are restated in English classes and Sunday pulpits as Eternal Verities. The above sentiments recently came to me spun into gold in the form of a recalled calligraphy sample belonging to our friend, lately, sadly departed, Lucy Grimm. It said, "Art is the demonstration that the ordinary is extraordinary." I began to extrapolate art by this definition to include not only things in gilt frames or on marble pedestals, but also the very way you get through the day as well. Rabbi Hesh Sommer once shared with me a quote to the effect that we walk, unseeingly, amidst miracles every day.

I was feeling forlorn about my "so-called job" lately. After working at some prestigious bakeries, I was now a counterperson at a tacky soft-serve ice cream store in an ugly shopping mall. I felt chagrined rolling bubblegum swirl kiddie cones in rainbow sprinkles. My work life was tawdry and ordinary.

That it might be otherwise first occurred to me with the parting comment from the state health inspector (we passed). He told me, "You've got a good job; you make people happy." I contrasted this with the inspector's own job, where his appearance at a jobsite elicits mainly anxious scrambling – "Get that mop off the floor! Put your hairnet on!" I considered employees in, say, a dentist's office, where "customers" enter anticipating molar extractions, root canals and bills for a thousand dollars. I once watched a TV feature about an Oklahoma factory where interviewed workers equivocated about the "necessity" of making bombs to drop on Iraq.

But I also remembered an interview with comedian Robert Klein, whose career probably includes many long nights in sleazy, smoky dives. However, Klein saw his work as a high calling. What better job could you have on this Earth, he asked, than making people laugh? Likewise, I realized that no one for whom I made a banana split ever frowned. My job began to seem…extraordinary.

Still, I lamented my job site, where garish décor and walls plastered with kitschy ad posters fairly defined UU Malvina Reynolds's "ticky-tacky." Then I gazed through the storefront's large picture windows to regain my sense of place. I'd read an article about how workers with window views fared better productively and emotionally than those who couldn't see the world outside. Across the street, I could see trees all now in white and pink bloom. Above them wheeled two seagulls, emblematic of the New England I'd loved since I was a five year-old on vacation on Cape Cod, and where I now live. Wow.

I clocked out and stepped out to the parking lot. Though hardly a (Unitarian) Frank Lloyd Wright design, the lot did afford one of the few unimpeded views of the sky dome still left in my overdeveloped shoreline town. I beheld the Himalayas clouds billowing, towering directly over me. I strolled to my car. I thought of UU Christopher Reeve, lying on his traction bed, straining to wiggle a toe and for whom my casual amble must seem a breathtaking epiphany. I started my car at the end of just an ordinary day. Quite extraordinary.

# VIEWING HENRIETTA

My next-door neighbor for more than 30 years died recently. A chain-smoking alcoholic, she'd been weakened by lung cancer and emphysema. Her adult son discovered her, arms folded, sitting in a dining room chair; her heart, and apparently her spirit for life, had given out the previous day. On the table next to her rested the rulers of her life, a glass of wine and a half-smoked cigarette. In a final stroke of good fortune, the cigarette had gone out before igniting the house surrounding her.

My mother asked me to accompany her to what is euphemistically called "the viewing" at the funeral home. With some reluctance, I obliged. The experience was a cold water-splash reminder of just how uncomfortable I am with many mores and rituals of mainstream society. My different-drummer soul is like some rare-blooming flower; it seems to blossom only once each week, on Sunday mornings at SUUS. I remained tightly closed to everything at this viewing, which seemed designed to pretend that reality was other than what it was, that Henrietta's death had not occurred.

Ever the chipper back slappers, her two sons greeted us cheerfully. Amid small talk about what we'd all been up to lately, the older son asked (rhetorically, not pausing for any honest answer), "Didn't they do a great job on Mom? Except for the little trouble they had with her mouth..." I looked at their mother's dead body, laid inside a burnished, dark wood casket. By technicians who had never known her, Henrietta's body had been clothed in a best dress, the hair stiffly coiffed and the face heavily made up. Her brown plastic-rimmed glasses rested over her closed, sightless eyes. Someone said, "It's just like she's asleep." I no more bought this deception than I bought the theology of those who knelt on the velvet cushion and crossed themselves, feeling consoled that Henrietta was up there with her Savior Jesus. Nor could I decide whether the sons' casual ebullience was some chin-up denial or emotional myopia. The whole room seemed garish and artificial.

To me, this dysfunctional viewing room was emblematic of our society's dysfunctional attitude about how to treat the dead. How much more direct, honest and simple does flame seem to me. Once the part of a human body that animated it as a unique individual who laughed, cried and loved as only that one could, once that personality, that spirit – that soul – has left its body, what matters the remaining flesh corpse? Why not consign that body to fire and so return it to Nature as elemental gases and an ash residue to nourish the Earth where the body spent its spirit-inhabited life? In many cultures cremation is traditional and it's increasingly chosen here.

An even more visceral return of bodies to Nature is the practice in other cultures of leaving the dead outside so birds and other animals can partake of the body as food. I once read a review of a television documentary on Tibet that cautioned parents about "possible disturbance to children" if they viewed a scene depicting this practice. But would these parents be concerned to have the kids watch a Nature program that showed a lion eating an antelope or a bear eating a salmon? Do these parents give the kids dead chickens and cows for dinner? Isn't it all the same natural cycle of dead animals sustaining living animals? By the way, when the family goes to church, isn't the communion wafer supposed to be the flesh of the body of Christ?

When the living personality that is me, Richard, leaves the body holding this pen, I would have no qualms if

48

the body became dinner for an eagle. But I'd prefer that this body's ashes enable the SUUS memorial garden to bloom for another year. I think of how Henrietta's chemically preserved body, inside its thousand-dollar box, will join millions of others like it, to be sunk under the soil of large tracts of immobilized land. Ironically, the outcome will all be the same anyhow – eventually box and body will break down; both will become food for small, wriggly animals and so will nourish the dirt of Earth.

Sorry, now I'm confused. Tell me again – which are the civilized beings and which ones the barbarians?

# LIFE IS … OH YES, FOR LIVING

Recently, I underwent a religious conversion. I didn't find Jesus (nor He me), nor did I receive a visitation from the Holy Virgin. Rather, I erased a gloomy attitude by actually practicing some UU premises that I prescribe to others with such glib ease. Ours is, indeed, a demanding faith to adhere to because we count more how you actually live your life than what you say in proper settings.

Since my former partner, Nancy, moved to Virginia, I've felt vulnerable for lack of an extra pair of hands and a second opinion in emergencies. On the analyst's couch, I suppose I might own that since my mother left my father and me in the summer after my $11^{th}$ birthday, I have, at my core, been searching for someone to resume taking care of me. Living alone, I had gradually circumscribed my travels to where driving the 18 miles to New Haven was an odyssey to the edge of my Earth. Loath to admit it, I was becoming like Dylan Thomas' maiden Auntie Bessie, who whimpered at the sideboard [of Life] because she had already been frightened, twice, by a clockwork mouse.

So increasing trepidation overcame me after I accepted my eighty-seven year old Uncle Tom's invitation to meet him in Manhattan and see a movie I'd already committed myself to leading a discussion about at church. Ironically, I once gave a talk at church called, "Optimism: Notes From a Recovering Pessimist." I had fallen off the optimism wagon with a thud. Lately, my imagination was at its most fertile, conjuring worst-case scenarios. Clockwork mouse? The Big Apple was more like Clockwork Orange! If I escaped four possible flat tires getting to New Haven, I could still get lost and/or miss the train. If I somehow survived to Grand Central Station, crazed mugger gangs could beat me to a puddle as I set foot off the train. Or maybe I'd be spared till I descended into the hell-tube of the subway, where a deinstitutionalized mental patient would promptly push me to incineration on the third rail. While I wasn't quite whimpering at the sideboard, I left to begin my "enjoyable day" with my mouth set, unsmiling, and the storm-warning flags were flying full-mast inside my head.

Driving clench-fisted to Union Train Station, I diverted myself by singing some old hymns we've sung at church. One said "My country is the world," and another, "...and all men [sic] are my kin." I recalled that our old hymnal is titled, "Hymns For the *Celebration* (not the Endurance!) of Life." Hadn't I said in my own optimism sermon, "Life should be an adventure, not an ordeal"? I picked my train seat and determined to relax into thinking the world a friendly place.

The next thing I knew, a familiar-looking man got on at Westport and sat across from me. Deciding I'd regret not asking, I leaned over and said, "I don't mean to intrude, but are you...?" Well, he was: the music/social critic, Nat Hentoff, whose writing I'd admired for years. I shook hands and told him so; from my new perspective, the adventure had begun.

Safe in Grand Central, I gaped at an exhibit of artist Lisa Lou's 20-foot square sculpture of an entire backyard scene crafted from thirty million – thirty million – minuscule beads. She said gluing them for four years was "a meditation, a prayer," and I gushed my awe and joy to complete strangers next to me. The demons must have Saturdays off from subway duty. I found myself flowing along comfortably in the underground stream of people of varied sizes, colors and languages, who were all intent on pretty much the same things: keeping their kids in tow, keeping what they ate off their clothes and focusing on which station was *their* stop.

The movie theater was on 12th street, the street where my parents lived when I was born, and after I met Uncle Tom he escorted me to see the old brownstone (fifth floor walk-up, no elevator) where this life adventure of mine began fifty-three years ago. The movie, while absorbing, was almost anticlimactic after all the enjoyment I'd been getting out and about in the real world.

Going home, I eyed the passing landscape through the train window, watching while Harlem gradually became Greenwich. Along the shoreline towns, I noted one, two, three cemeteries. I reminded myself that I wasn't in one of them yet, that I was still taking my turn at being alive on this Earth. Not to be busy making the most of my turn seemed a sacrilege against my religion.

# LANDSCAPE WITH A FIGURE

I went to see some paintings on exhibit in New Haven. Whether I simply thought I'd enjoy myself or whether my behavior was guided by genes inherited from my artist father, I'm not sure. I suppose the two motivations are intertwined in my helixes. I was aware that the paintings I enjoyed most were 1940s realist landscapes done in a style my father had also adopted. In fact the picture I responded to most favorably was a winter cityscape, a brown and russet mosaic of roofs, facades, walls and porches, outlined in black and blocked with areas of snow white. The painting's sole figure stood in front of a wall; a featureless man, characterized only by a long oval head with a high forehead widow's peak – both of which my father possessed.

As I stared at the brush-sketched figure, my mind drifted romantically. "I'll bet that man *is* Dad," I thought. "Dad's spirit has returned from 'somewhere' and he's saying hello right from that canvas on the wall. He's here in this gallery to renew our bond of enjoying art together and to comfort me."

Then my mind broke in on its own reverie. "That's (barnyard expletive), Richard," it snapped. "Your father died 30-odd years ago. You kissed his corpse goodbye, watched the coffin get buried and that was the end of Edward C. Gressley. Period."

When I was nine or ten years old, I concluded that I didn't – couldn't – really believe the supernatural Bible stories that adults were teaching me on Sunday mornings. With some trepidation, I asked my parents' permission to stop attending Sunday School, and they, assuming I was being true to my own conscience, granted it.

Years later I entered a period when I sustained myself with my reinvention of classical Heaven as a personalized paradise where I'd reunite with (now dead) Dad, as well as stroll and chat with my own gods, Monet, Jefferson, Beethoven. But ensuing years, with the disappointments and setbacks they bring us all, made it increasingly hard to maintain such idylls in the face of gritty reality. Eventually I let go of my romantic notions, as an adolescent puts aside a Mother Goose picture book.

My open-question agnosticism was veering past deism, which at least postulates a disinterested, absentee-parent Creator of the Universe. My opinions (a synonym for beliefs) were headed for outright atheism. God and an Afterlife were solely projections of our own primitive limbic brainstem's urges and desires for power and nurture. If a physicist's equation couldn't prove it, it didn't exist. There's no one Out There and dead is dead.

Just one thing – my reductionist universe was a cold and severe place. I might have made my beliefs unassailable logically, but I'd drained them emotionally. They provided me no comfort, and isn't that one of the primary functions of religion? By contrast, I did take pleasure and solace in the times when, for instance, I browsed our own hymnbook. The song lyrics and prose passages there spoke of hope, courage, love and joy – things not quantifiable, that can't be proved mathematically or forensically. They are, nonetheless, vital vectors in the sum of our humanity; they were the missing factors in my equation of Reality.

Besides, how final was the word of the scientists anyway? Up until the recent last century, they told us reality was delimited by three dimensions. After Albert Einstein's arrival on Earth, they expanded reality to include a fourth dimension of time. Lately, physicists are starting to postulate a "reality" (by now, quotation marks are compulsory) of as many as nine dimensions, ten dimensions. So, who are they (let alone I!) to know whether my father might not be happily ensconced in one of those kaleidoscopic dimensions (painting what new landscapes now?!) and even dropping back here for an occasional visit?

Whether any of this was, indeed, true wasn't the point, I decided. The very fact that the painted figure had started me thinking about my father, something I hadn't done for some time, was an end in itself and all I needed to know. As is my wont, before I left the gallery, I returned for one last view of the work I'd enjoyed the most. I gazed at the man in the painting, nodded and silently said so long to Dad.

# STAYING PUT

Driving home with milk, broccoli and cat food last week, I caught sight of a house I'd never seen before. Its weathered stone façade told me this was no nouveau riche mansion thrown up a month ago. It was, indeed, someone's home that had stood there for more years than I'd been tooling by oblivious to it. Thirty-two years I've lived here. Never noticed it. My small town is still revealing itself to me.

In print and via airwaves, I've encountered many laments uttered for the circumscribed, deprived lives of various rustics who've never ventured beyond five miles from their birth villages, as if Jules Verne's Phileas Fogg were the only Compleat Person. I could never deny the grandeur and majesty our planet offers to behold, but I also wonder just how blighted are lives that may have missed

"the Las Vegas experience" or the grandeur and majesty of Love Canal, NY. With the onset of middle age realism, I've come to accept that there are just some places I'll never see. As Yale's Harold Bloom said about (ahem) the Internet, "It's like Congo's jungle – I know it exists, but I know I'll never go there." Besides, in Eastern religious traditions, the question is posed whether it is better to climb a hundred mountains once or to climb one mountain a hundred times. Herein, a few words favoring that single peak.

Staying in one place fosters a sense of stewardship, of caring for your own backyard. Where I grew up in New Jersey, the house next to ours was never less cared for than when it was rented for six months by an itinerant Air Force family. They seemed not to mind how much mess they made because they endlessly decamped for clean-slate new houses in different states.

With your roots sunk in one place, you absorb a sense of identity with your acre of Earth. In a tumultuous world, I for one, cherish some reliableness. But steadfast is not petrified. In the generation I've lived here, my town has not been fixed in amber. Where I now cross an asphalt parking lot, I once stood in tall grass at dusk, eating Maple Shade ice cream, while a skunk (which seemed as oblivious of me as I was of that stone house) nuzzled an empty banana barge dish by my feet. I myself now work inside four walls scooping ice cream in a mall store. But could I board a time machine to thrust me backward from now to

then, those four walls would disappear as would the rest of the mall and I'd be left standing in the open air strawberry fields where I knelt to pick-my-own 32 Junes ago.

From my back door landing, I can see the same crescent moon that lovers atop the Eiffel Tower spoon under or climbers on Everest view through shaded goggles. In Guilford, my skin absorbs from our Sun the same

warmth and vitamin D as it would in Vienna or Buenos Aires. Our Earth was created as an egalitarian globe and visitors from some interstellar elsewhere would see no one place raised on any apex of special favor.

A place is more than just an empty stage set; it is peopled with a cast of characters – primarily, for me, the SUUS family. This abiding group is my social bedrock, but it is hardly static, never stultifying. No need to chase far-flung parades; the parade comes to me. Where 20 or 30 once met in a living room, now more than a hundred gather in a sanctuary that didn't exist 20 years ago. I've watched as children became adults, and no few adults (some elderly, some sadly not) departed in death. When I attended my first SUUS service, our current president was yet to be born.

In a hyper world of hot new places, I could be called a social/urban as well as a technological Luddite, wanting everyone to remain like the provincials of (Hamden resident and UU) Thornton Wilder's "Our Town." Well, I plead guilty. I cherish as eternal that play's homely verities. The truths told to its characters in their hundred trips up the metaphorical mountain of Grover's Corners, New Hampshire, dependably bring me to tears – tears of appreciation for life.

# MABOROSI

I have set a rule for myself here not to comment on polemics and current events, feeling I lacked sufficient knowledge and authority to set myself up as an arbiter and problem solver. But I have not been on some other planet (though in my life I often feel like I come from one!) and thus unaware of what happened last September 11. As with all other humans with hearts, my thoughts and feelings were brought low by that sad, sad day. To plumb my emotions, I watched a Japanese movie called "Maborosi," a visual meditation on loss.

It's the story of a young mother whose husband was killed by a train while he walked on the railroad tracks. Whether he heard the train yet continued to walk anyway is an unanswered question. She enters an arranged marriage to a widowed father and the story chronicles her progress and setbacks in moving on with her life. I found the film not only deeply moving but stunning to behold as well. Each camera shot was a painterly still life; not only artfully composed interior scenes, but also seemingly random, homely exteriors of overgrown railroad yards or rundown industrial buildings – thus demonstrating the spiritual truth of the hanging in Lucy Grimm's home: "Art is the demonstration that the ordinary is extraordinary." But this is another story.

To the point, in one scene the woman stands by the ocean and rants in frustration at why her late husband didn't get off the tracks. Her new husband replies that the sea is very beguiling. He says that once his father, out in his fishing boat, saw a "maborosi" – a strange light far out at sea. This image is left poetically unexplored further – leaving that to the viewer. Did the father pursue the light, knowing it could be dangerous, or did he decide just to leave it alone and tend to his fishing?

I thought of the thousands who lost loved ones without resolution in the crash sites and building rubble. Will endless wonderings, ceaseless "what if…" and "if only…" become their maborosi? Will preoccupied pursuit lead them farther and farther out in trackless emotional waters and cast their lives hopelessly adrift? Or will they, like Jews at the end of shiva, be able to declare an end to mourning and questioning, and so return to casting the fishing lines of their own lives?

September 11 left me only vicariously bereft, but it caused to glow ever brighter my personal maborosi. I pondered, with renewed, intense anguish, whether God exists – the unanswered question which has drawn my mind by its nose (if my mind *has* a nose!) for most of my life. Perhaps I should yield to the wisdom of Thomas Jefferson, who said, "When I meet with a proposition beyond finite comprehension, I abandon it as I do a weight which human strength can not lift, and I think ignorance, in these cases, is truly the softest pillow on which I can lay my head." And even the limbo of irresolution has its benefits. As writer Nick Tosches said, "The deeper we seek, the deeper we descend from knowledge to mystery, which is the only place where wisdom abides."

# SAY WHEN ... PLEASE

Hear my cry and my prayer, O God! What is enough?

I sent a small check to help Turkish earthquake relief efforts. It was quite small – I'm sure I could have managed more without jeopardizing the roof over my *own* head. In a recent New York Times magazine essay, Princeton University ethicist Peter Singer told me it's morally incumbent upon me to give a *lot* more than I did. What is enough? I do a little volunteer work. I shelve books in the library and I work at the food bank. Perhaps the burdens of some (few) others are thus lightened, but I'm no Mother Teresa. Should I be? Wasn't hers the level of commitment to our fellows that Jesus urged us to? My conscience whispers "yes." What idealism I have tells me there is some minimum level of "enough" for our good works, and that we are accountable if we fall below it.

While my conscience provides an answer to my own question, my middle age is perplexed by a diminishing tendency (among many diminishing tendencies) to feel cocksure about anything. What I now view as that arrogance is increasingly replaced by a "what if they just happen to be right?" consideration afforded those holding unlikely, or unlikable, opinions. Now, what if, say, the philosopher Nietzsche is right and we live in the universe he described: barren of God and empty of meaning? Then my question will go unanswered because there is no one, no God, to answer it. "What is enough?" is a moot question if our conscience, whose bite Nietzsche called "indecent," is nothing more than an invention of our own masochism, a hair shirt of the mind. The sense of "ought" or "should" is a manufactured weight of guilt thumped upon our straining shoulders by – ahem – organized religions of all stripes. But is *that* the answer I want?

With similar frustration do I enjoy the beauties of this life. And ample joy on this Earth I have – from the sight of sky-touching sequoia forests and illuminated Notre Dame across the night Seine, to the evolution of love I experienced over 16 years with Nancy. Such things have made my heart race and my eyes brim with grateful tears. But now I'm home from Marin County and Paris, Nancy has moved to Virginia, and I wonder whether my fast pulse and tears were sufficient appreciation. What's more, I ask if there exists somewhere a reality to appreciate that is still unknown to me. I have never had a transcendent experience that carried my senses literally out of my mind or body.

Just as I fret to consider that Nietzche *could* be right, that there is "nothing more," so too, I yearn to believe, as did the Transcendentalists I claim as my forebears, that indeed there *is* "something more." I romance the notion that *something* even grander lies veiled behind/ beyond the bright sunsets, waterfalls and starry nights that swell my heart as large as it can get in this current life. One of my favorite images is a 19$^{th}$-century woodcut of a man, like a boy popping his head outside the circus tent, whose torso has pierced through the membrane of this world of hills, trees and sky to behold the light rays, suns and wheels of that Something More beyond. But Doubting Thomas is Richard. I have stepped outside this earthly membrane only metaphorically, never literally through my senses. To say I have would be wistful pretending, and my embrace of those who claim they have is withheld due to my niggling concern that they, too, may be wistful pretenders to the point of self-delusion. Maybe their raptures of The Beyond are only the imaginings of this world lofted by purpler prose than mine. Still, I'm not cocksure.

66

Thus do I lift my plea unto Thee, O God!…Silence.

# APPROACHING THE END:
## A SOLIPSIST'S VIEW

Kim's recent Sunday morning remarks about life's "winter" years generated in me (as usual) many a self-absorbed thought. If, in sharing some here, any chords are struck or bells rung, I shan't have navel-gazed in vain.

As we age, it's only realistic to anticipate increasing malfunctions of the body and the mind/spirit. At fifty-six, I've yet to endure any major instances of the former, but I've made up for this by getting a prodigy's early start on the latter. A hymnbook reading tells us the secret of vitality: it's the spiritual capacity to keep *zest* in living. Now, zest has never come to my angst-knotted cerebrum without strenuous effort. However, another thought, from writer Heywood Hale Broun, consoles me. There will come a time, he said, when passion and ambition are both gone. Curiosity will sustain you.

My earlier life's passions are already mere dying embers and, except for wanting to own a Martin guitar (achieved), I never had much ambition anyway. But if curiosity is what it takes, I should be okay. I delighted in a recent TV profile of a cell biologist who, at 102, still goes to work every day (someone else drives) "to find out the next thing." And I come from good stock here; my mother, approaching eighty-five, is still as avid a reader as any I know, and my newly ninety year-old uncle still attends lectures and readings all around Manhattan. As I grow older and discover ever more things I don't know, the list of books I want to read, films see, music hear, grows commensurately. I cite again a favorite talking blues lyric: "…the only reason I stick around at all is just to see what's gonna happen next." Curiosity will sustain me.

But death, inevitably, does come to us each and all. Emotionally, I flatter (delude?) myself that I remain decades away from staring into death's eyes. Intellectually, I have reached a limited understanding with the specter. I reason that after we die either there is something or there is nothing. If nothing, I might liken death to the soundest sleep – no bad fate in a sleep-deprived society. If something, I imagine "it" could be either worse than or equal to/better than this life. Universalist doctrine (an oxymoron?) rejects afterlife punishment so I discount any worse hereafter. If equal to, I've been relatively blessed here on Earth; if better than, well, the best yet awaits me.

Jean-Paul Sartre said there are two ways to go to the gallows: as a hero or as a coward. Since death is inexorable, why not embrace it with accepting grace rather than gnashing teeth? When my own death is at hand, I hope I can exit with the class articulated by UU minister Peter Fleck's granddaughter. She told him she saw dying as something like leaving a happy party and saying, "Thank you – I've had a lovely time, and now I must be going home." I find it telling that the lovely, soothing largo movement of Dvorak's New World Symphony, often played as a balm for someone's death, is referred to as "Going Home." And I believe it is not only poetically satisfying, but also scientifically correct that we come from the same place of origin as everything else in the entire Universe. Thus, in going home, we would be journeying to be at one again with all the rest of Creation. What greater adventure, what happier prospect can there be?

# CONVEYANCES

My old Ford Escort died about three years ago. It was stolid, conservative and oh, so respectable; a boxy squareback in dark "English racing green" which, in the fifties, my parents had redubbed "Gressley green" because that was always the color of the cars we bought. It died driving down I-95 when the timing belt broke, irreparably bending the piston rods. This happened while I was taking my elderly, disoriented mother to the doctor's for what was euphemistically termed "a checkup"...but that's another story...

Following six months of unemployment, I had recently gotten a new job, so I needed a replacement car to get me to work. Bentleys were out of the question. A budgetary ceiling of $2,000 in cash simplified the selection process wonderfully. Following a hasty canvass of local used car lots, the choice was made: a silver '83 Honda Accord which, if it were a house, would have been described as "needs work."

It had on it 86,000 miles...plus some other things: a body splotched with malignant tumors of rust; seats that, though actually threadbare from wear, nevertheless looked as though they'd been slashed with a knife; an unlatchable glove-compartment door that forever rested in the front passenger's lap, and a transmission that turned accelerating into a ever-worsening seizure of spasmodic bucking...to name but a few.

Several hundred dollars more fixed (replaced) the transmission, but not my attitude. Driving this thing, I felt conspicuously like a poor country cousin, and certainly no longer "respectable." Eventually I realized that, since I wasn't about to spend another two grand to eliminate the source of my stress, I ought to change my attitude toward the stress. Making lemonade out of this lemon, I started cultivating a more devil-may-care stance. I came to relish my Indiana Jones insouciance and ultimately drove my rattletrap with a certain damn-the-torpedoes, ain't-we-havin'-fun glee. And, bottom line – the car has lasted twice as long as I expected it to and continues to do all I ever wanted it to: it gets me from here to there with down-to-earth reliability and efficiency.

As a coda (and hoping the metaphor is not too Billy Graham), I venture to add that I suffered no such discomfiture when I traded in my religious faith. The boxy "Gressley green" Protestantism of my childhood died many years ago. Happily, my spirit was under no such financial constraints; the Unitarian Universalism I took as my replacement was of the very highest quality I could find. Never for an instant did I feel as if I had "traded down." I relished, indeed, I felt my soul was defined by the conspicuousness – the irreverence – of being outside the theological mainstream. Bottom line on this replacement – it has lasted the rest of my life thus far and it continues to do all I ever wanted it to: it conveys my spirit along the journey with down-to-earth reliability and efficiency.

# LOVED ONES

I never thought of myself as an animal lover in particular. This stems partly, I think, from the childhood allergies that prevented me from having pets while growing up. I did have some guppies once, but they were not eminently huggable. Also, I think their cosmic consciousness was skewed to where they thought they were lemmings, for they wound up jumping en masse out of the fishbowl to their deaths.

Better than a dime for a candy bar (circa 1957), my best friend Ronnie's and my favorite treat from my commercial-artist father used to be a large sheet of paper from his sketch pad for each of us. We'd float the pages down to the living room floor, hunch ourselves over them on our knees and cover them with drawings.

Even then, man was the measure of all things for me, for I was always trying to render the twists and turns of the human form. My humans were always male – and surprising to me now – they were always being hacked by Viking swords or skewered by Apache arrows. Next to my mayhem, I thought Ronnie's sketches were quite dull and odd. Ronnie was always drawing ducks landing on a pond or deer feeding in a forest clearing.

To quote the Shakespeare of my late teens, Bob Dylan, "Ah, but I was so much older then, I'm younger than that now." The other day, I took stock of my bedroom dresser top (quite messy), and realized that where other people have framed portraits of beloved spouses, children and parents, I have color photos of pigs, blue-footed boobies, sea cows and goats. I've come to where these faces are the ones I prefer to meet my gaze. They can improve my spirit(s) as few humans can.

The goofy eyes and turquoise feet of the booby birds, and the mud-caked and dripping snouts of the pigs can lighten my darkest gloom. The steadfastness of the goats atop Montana mountain peaks, and the paradoxical grace of the lumpish manatees soothe the anxieties which, I'm afraid, I avidly collect.

But maybe an animal lover always dwelled somewhere in me. Hanging on the wall behind the dresser is an old watercolor of my father's, which my mother tells me was painted from life. It portrays me as a child of four from behind, on a bridge, standing on tiptoe to see, over the railing, a snow-white egret standing in the small canal. It is a depiction of wonderment.

# GHOSTS: THE LIGHTS

I once dwelt at column's length here on the skylight in our meeting room. But when I lower my gaze slightly, my eyes light (no pun intended) on what, to me is the true cynosure of our "sacred space," the overhead lights. These fixtures, which illuminate our services at least in the physical sense, are merely eight incandescent light bulbs behind rice paper shades. But what shades! These paper panels, five per bulb, surround and embrace the lights like graceful fans, yet they also jut boldly into the surrounding space like sails, wings. Spiritually, they evoke in me the sails of Columbus' three ships which, defying their times' conventional wisdom, sailed off in search of truth. If I welcome visitors to our services, I say, "G'morning, how are you?" but my unspoken thoughts cry, "Look up at our lights!"

Still, I have no intrinsic fetish for light bulbs or rice paper. Every Sunday morning when I behold the fixtures, I inevitably conjure memories of those of us who installed those lights. Nearly two decades ago, many members scurried through the empty, newly-built room to help the architect, then-member Louis Mackall, put the finishing touches on things. We climbed scaffolds and ladders to complete the light shades and I, for one, felt like an apprentice artisan working in the Sistine Chapel under Michelangelo. Noting today the occasional small wrinkles and crooked cut edges of the rice paper, I think back those 20 years and still remember Louie's assurances to us who cut and stapled the paper that if the shades were not perfectly drumhead-taut and ruler-straight, it would not matter. Maybe Louie felt pressure from deadlines; maybe by that point he just wanted to be done with it. Or perhaps he was following the Shaker quilters who, on purpose, sewed a mistake into each of their patchworks to demonstrate that they, unlike God, were not perfect.

No matter. We all folded and stapled cheerfully. Don and Bruce, Nancy and Lucy, Marylyn and Gene. We were all of those 20 years younger then. Our hair was darker and thicker, and we were all vital with enthusiasm. Since then, our inquiries into life have led some elsewhere. For some, their time of life is over and they are gone from us forever.

But while they were here, they laughed and listened, danced and sang, debated and wept among us in that room, and each time I look up at our lights, I see wispy traces of them on their scaffold and ladder rigging. At Gettysburg, Abraham Lincoln said he could not consecrate that ground; the soldiers who had fought there had already done that. Just so, I named our meeting room "sacred space," but I did not make it so. Otherwise just a cube of wood and sheetrock, it is made sacred by the lingering presence of those who once filled it. Each one of those ghosts is indeed holy.

# GERSHWIN WAS WRONG;
## THE LIVIN' *AIN'T EASY*

Hemingway put the gun to his head and fired. So did Van Gogh. Sylvia Plath took the gas; Virginia Woolf walked into the river. Alcoholism washed away Dylan Thomas and William Faulkner, two among *many* other writers (a complete list of whom would overflow a score of these newsletters.) Handel was a textbook case of manic depression. William Styron wrote a best seller recounting *his* depression. By these standards, Beethoven, "merely" an irascible grump, was a paragon of healthy emotional adjustment.

Some people dance with life. Creative souls wrestle with it. One study showed creative people are 35 times more likely to seek psychological help – help in coping with life – than the average person. For the artist, the very act of existing, of *being*, is hard. An intimate friend described the poet Rilke as "often tormented by his own physical existence." Philosopher Isiah Berlin, speaking of author Edmund Wilson, said, "he was an uncomfortable man, uncomfortable with himself... he was not bland, he was the opposite of being peaceful... it was difficult for him; life was difficult and writing was difficult." In a New Yorker cartoon, a woman comments to her visitor about her husband, who is seated before them with a look of consternation. She says, "Living brings up a lot of issues for him." I took the husband to be an artist. I also took his name to be Richard.

For me as well, existing is no cakewalk. Whether this ipso facto puts me in the company of artists is a decidedly open question, but in my life I've meandered down myriad creative avenues. As a child, I pencil-sketched, emulating my artist father. For 40 years, I've tried to play the guitar (one day I'll get it). I've baked and decorated cakes as a livelihood. Now (no snickering, please), I'm writing these essays. I take Barbara Carlson's description of my writing style as "quirky" (read "tortuous syntax") as evidence that, as Beatle Ringo sang, "you know it don't come easy." I once complained to Barbara that writing these columns was like pulling impacted molars. She quoted me Thomas Mann's observation that a writer is someone for whom writing is more difficult than it is for other people.

Why such perturbation? Maybe it's a necessary impetus for change – for creation. Were the oyster not irritated by the sand grain, it would produce no pearls. Maybe it's even a *desirable* ingredient in creation's recipe. Sculptor Agustus Saint-Gaudens said, "What garlic is to salad, insanity is to art."

Some psychologists theorize that our whole lives are a quest to return to a state of mystical unity we enjoyed before birth. Perhaps the creative simply feel a stronger tug of this yearning. Of Rilke, that friend said that he longed to transcend mortality. In "Vincent," Don McLean sang of Van Gogh, "This world was never meant for one as beautiful as you." In his "God Loves A Drunk" (in the "holy fool" tradition?), British Sufi folk-rocker (not a misprint) Richard Thompson sings, "A drunk's only trying to get free of his body, and soar like an eagle high up there in Heaven."

Yes, what joy to burst from the Laocoon entanglements of this life. To paraphrase Mann, artists are those for whom existing is more difficult than it is for other people.

# BE YOU (GOES FOR ME, TOO)

I was struck and saddened by the death in a plane crash of U.S. Senator Paul Wellstone. I lamented the loss of one of the few remaining political voices of 1960s idealism (my own remnants of which I still clutch at). And I was struck with great admiration for the tributes to him, from liberals and conservatives both, as a thoroughly *authentic* person. This is rare praise among politicians who, depending on their chicken-dinner audience du jour, usually try to please (I think Abraham Lincoln said "fool") all the people all the time.

Lincoln pointed out the futility of trying to please/fool all people always. But it takes strength, *guts*, to be authentic. Being authentic will inevitably cause a politician to alienate *some* constituents. For any of us to be our genuine selves will contradict the wishes of some parent, teacher, boss, priest – or society at large. I think many of us spend all our maturing years negotiating a compromise between who we really are and who others expect us to be. But eventually, as years lived tip the scale more heavily than years left, we must ask ourselves: whose life am I living – theirs or mine?

Personal authenticity is virtually an article of faith for us conscientious UUs, who joke that we're bad hymn singers because we're always reading ahead to see if we agree with the lyrics. I recall a New Yorker cartoon (now *which* file folder did I shove that into?) of a man who, in cocktail party chit-chat, says, "That's where the Unitarians and I part company; I see nothing wrong with living a lie." At SUUS, our Sunday Service meetings sometimes bog down deepest when we start to fret too much over what some hypothetical first-time visitor from Main Street might think if they walked in on somebody's unorthodox (innovative) proposal for a Sunday Service.

It seems true that two of our most vaunted forebears, Emerson and (unofficially) Thoreau, are championed precisely because of their uncompromising, damn-the-torpedoes integrity. But I do note that unbending honesty can have a dark side: a certain impolitic bluntness which can grate more than it persuades. Perhaps we all know someone whose brass-knuckles directness causes guests to keep a wary distance from them at coffee hour.

"Nothing is harder to become than the person you always claimed to be." Maybe we all need petite delusions to lubricate our way over sandpaper reality. We might regard ourselves as "blond," not "gray," when the blond pours out of a bottle. At 220 pounds, we might call ourselves "burly" or "plus-size," instead of "heavy." Or maybe we imagine ourselves open-minded when we'd really just as soon boycott Jesse Helms rather than listen to his argument.

Perhaps, like many ideals, authenticity is a goal on the horizon to be continually striven – struggled – for. May we all move toward it. I've let go of thinking that I have more hair left than I do, though I'm still working on seeing myself not as "slim" but as " unhealthily underweight." My boss at work once told me, "You've got your own style, Rich." I cherish that as a compliment. Now if only I could get those endless tape loops of the Rat Pack's "My Way" and "I've Got to Be Me" out of my head.

# LUDDITE ON THE LOOSE (AGAIN)

My only contacts with our denominational parent, the Unitarian Universalist Association, are numerous fund solicitations I receive in the mail (I forget if I ever answered one) and The World magazine, similarly received (I forget if I ever finished one). I have never heard the UUA spoken of affectionately in the hallowed administrative halls of SUUS – though I should keep in mind the "rep" our congregation has for ornery cantankerousness (which I do my small part to uphold proudly). However, I must at least grant the UUA prescience. Back in the mid-eighties (it was sometime during my incarnation as the La Cuisine baker), the UUA chose as the theme for the national General Assembly, "On Staying Human In the Computer Age."

The computer age was barely off Bill Gates's drawing board then (home computers were the exception, not the rule), but already the UUA saw the pixel writing on the wall – er, screen.

Recently, film critic Roger Ebert lamented the paradoxical perfection of computer-generated special effects in movies. The illusions computers can now create are *so* virtually real, he contended, that, increasingly, audiences don't even realize what they're seeing is, indeed, a special effect and not reality itself. This blasé unawareness robs viewers of their human senses of awe and wonder. It was the very *im*perfection in the lumbering movements of King Kong and the Beast From 20,000 Fathoms that made us whisper appreciatively, "...ooh, wow!" Recall, by the way, what has been Hollywood's shorthand to depict nightmare future societies: the image is a gray honeycomb room of isolated workers all staring soullessly at...computer screens. Say – aren't those the same partitioned offices many of us Dilberts work in right now?

In the ice-cream store where I now work, birthday cakes with pictures on them are popular. We used to trace pictures onto the cakes and fill them in with colored gels. Kids, and no few parents, enjoyed the bright, homespun results. The human effort cost $2.75. No more. Now a computer reproduces the pictures in drab-colored perfection on an edible glucose sheet that's laid on the cake – for $8.00. True, the computer can reproduce family photos, but am I alone in thinking that slicing and eating your child's or parent's face is bizarre, vaguely macabre, atavistic and heavy with Freudian baggage?

UU minister Peter Fleck once wrote a book on the blessings of imperfection. Perfection is inimical to certain things, like birthday cakes or birthday and Christmas cards made by children – made by humans. Each Christmas lately, I receive some "Dear Everyone" letters in an artificial script produced by a computer. Will the great grandchildren of today's kids no longer be able to grasp and guide an archaic pen to fashion letters and words uniquely *theirs* and not a machine's?

In 1984 (roll over, George Orwell), the UUA voiced its caution during the opening salvos in this contest to retain our human souls. With the struggle's pitch ever-mounting today, these small (inconsequential?) dispatches from the front indicate that victory is far from won and may even be receding from sight. I felt that the bugler was about to sound retreat last week when I opened the UUA's latest fund request letter. Below "Sincerely," the writer's name was signed "Jane Smith." But the stiffly rendered signature, devoid of character, told me the writer was really Hewlett Packard.

## JUST WHEN YOU THOUGHT IT WAS SAFE TO READ THIS COLUMN AGAIN

"So, when are you going to get a computer?"

Mike Evans' eyes didn't meet mine. They remained locked on the screen of the church office computer. Nevertheless, his question was directed at me, the heretic.

I took it as the opening thrust in a fencing match.

I can almost feel the centrifugal spin from the collective roll of many readers' eyeballs in their heads - "Oh, no! There he goes again on this computer thing!" After I swore off any more technology-rant columns, yes, I plead guilty. I feel like a reformed drunk crawling back in the bottle, or like one Commander-in-Chief unable to resist certain bodily proclivities of his own. But technology is the biggest target out there in our 2000 world, and besides, I was provoked beyond restraint. Returning to the duel – I mean, conversation...

"Mike, why do I need a computer? Convince me."

"Well, for one, so you can get e-mail."

Ah, yes! So I can fill my day jumping and jerking in response to every trivial, passing thought and query from friends and family – not to mention advertisers.

Over two hundred years ago, the Founding Fathers invented a nationwide delivery system that brings reflective, hand-crafted letters – an art form – to my door daily. Later, Alexander Graham Bell devised a contraption (in my opinion, a decidedly mixed blessing) that provides more immediate communication, one that lets you hear and respond to the actual human voice of the communicant.

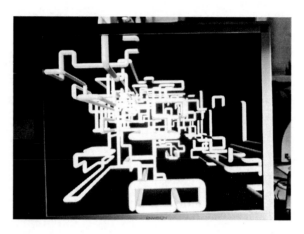

And consider this: when I open a letter or answer the phone, I don't risk exposing my house to some viral contagion that could destroy my financial records or blab my credit-card number to 50,000 strangers. As to the attraction of staying in 24-hour, constant touch with people, all this curmudgeon can do is recall his delight in an old radio skit by the comedy team, Bob and Ray.

Ray played some big business executive and his secretary, Bob, burst into his office. "Mr. Jones, guess what! Your long-lost brother, whom you haven't seen in twenty-five years, is waiting outside!" Ray groans, "Ooooh... now what does he want?"

Later, Mike parries, "You could look things up on the Internet." Not good enough for this child of Gutenberg. The public library is my home away from home. First, going to the library gets me out of the house. (A man in the news, who christened himself "dot-com-guy," has vowed to stay in an empty house for a year, using only his computer to provide all his needs. One commentator predicted he'll go nuts in three months.)

Granted, in Brave New 2000 the library has no choice but to command its own battery of computers for patrons' use. But as an aesthete, I cherish beautiful things, and the library arrays before me shelf after shelf of just such tangible objects, the products of the bookbinder's and illustrator's art. Book, beautiful book, shall I compare thee to a cathode ray tube? I think not. Now I am, I admit, a sloucher. I like to cozy up when I read. How can I scrunch back into a comfy easy chair with a good computer screen, let alone take a good computer screen to bed with me? If some information eludes me, I can seek help from, even have a chat with, a real live, human librarian. No need to plough into a 700-page operator's manual that holds all the allure of an algebra text. Finally, no – the curmudgeon does not find amusing the badly animated little puppy-dog icon that electronically yips at him if he hits the wrong key.

I have read of how some indigenous populations are wary of cameras, suspecting these mysterious machines of being stealers of souls. Once I was bemused by such "quaint" beliefs. But the more computers surround and close in on me, the more I think those folks are on to something.

# FOR VIRGINIA: CLICHÉS? NO ANSWERS

I didn't expect this. The recent death of my mother produced in me only scant tears and no hand wringing; I had become emotionally estranged from her many years ago. But since she died, I have, to my surprise, found myself drifting into thoughts about her state of being – or lack thereof? – in death. To those familiar with the many dark facets of my nature, I suppose this distraction will provoke not surprise but only a yawn.

I was truly startled by my last encounter with my mother two days before she died. All her life, she was plucky, even defiant, but on that day I found her sitting in her hospital room cowering, consumed by fear. I asked her what she was so afraid of, and she said, "The emptiness ... the nothingness." The stark, haunted look in her eyes quite unnerved me, and I really felt it possible she was seeing a vision of her own impending death. And, I wondered, is her vision accurate? For all the ages' supernatural traditions, from ancient Hinduism to the Resurrection to the New Age, is this truly what death is – nothingness?

Thus distracted, I went to visit my dear, rediscovered friend, Dick, whose partner (of *52 years*), Frank, died last year. Of course, our wide-wheeling conversation (as rewarding to me as SUUS Sunday discussions) did not resolve this matter; the nature of death remains "the grand secret." However, we raised a further issue: the finite memory – and lives – of those who survive. Amazingly, Dick said Frank was concerned lest Dick forget him (no chance!). But memory does fade. Musician Warren Zevon, before he died in his mid-fifties recorded a legacy song titled "Keep Me In Your Heart *For A While* (italics mine)." Two brothers (both in their nineties), a niece and I survive my mother and when we are gone, so will be all awareness that Virginia Mulvaney ever existed. Then she will join the uncounted billions of souls, once beloved, now anonymous, who ever trod this Earth.

Historical memory has alighted on certain random (?) lives for long-term retention. But legacy is a two-edged blade. Many destroyers, from Attila to Hitler, are recalled because of their awful deeds. And even those around whom great world religions grew – Jesus and Muhammad are prime examples – continue to be the cause of destruction and death today.

Of far better consequence to this Earth, I thought, are those unheralded lives whose works have somehow come down to enrich us today. Frank Lloyd Wright said, "Life is only worth living if you can make it more beautiful than when you found it." By this criterion, the immortals of Earth include the early human who stroked the bison images onto the Lascaux cave walls. Also an unknown ancient Chinese poet whose six lines, when read aloud today, caused an audience of children to go "...Ooo!"

Sometimes I think each of our lives is like an infinitesimal eye-blink flash of light in the Universe. The meaning of this flash is unknown, but it fascinates those who witness it. Recently I read writer Jan Benzel's remembrance of "The Gates," the long row of scaffold-hung, orange banners that artist Christo erected for one month in Central Park a year ago. What she wrote of those undulating flags, I thought, could as well describe every life ever lived on our planet: "They're gone now, of course; that was part of the plan. Magic isn't magic unless it disappears."

# OUTSIDERS

For several years, I've been fascinated by "outsider art." Outsider art includes paintings, sculpture and collages created by – no surprise – outsider artists. These creators are loosely defined as nonacademically–trained persons living apart from society or in worlds of their own, who produce visionary works without caring whether or not it is art. "Outsider" is casually applied to any self-taught artist working off the radar of the mainstream world.

For a while, I wondered if the category could be broadened to include "reclusive writers," in which case maybe I could sneak in under the flaps of the term's big tent. But, I decided, probably not, since I put nine times as much time and effort into being reclusive as I ever put into writing. I began to see, however, that while I may not be an outsider artist, I am my own outsider theologian and I belong to an honorable outsider religion.

A vivid childhood memory places me back in my 1951 kindergarten classroom. During "creative playtime," most of the other kinder played "kitchen" (girls) or "fire house" (boys – 1951, don't forget). Riding my imaginary horse, I, however, circled the room's periphery as some sort of Lone Ranger maverick, observing the others from a distance. Rather telling, wot? Was this a child who would line up obediently to let robed adults push his head under water and stick wafers in his mouth? A few years later, my mother found me lying by myself in the backyard grass and asked what I was doing. "Oh," I replied, "just thinking." Was this a child who would acquiesce when told that one supernatural being is simultaneously three supernatural beings, and no, it doesn't make sense and it can't be explained, but just believe it anyway?!

And so it seems preordained (to cop a religious *insider* term) that I would join those exceptional, in the dual senses of "few in number" as well as "distinguished" souls, the UUs. For centuries, our ranks have been filled by those who stood outside society to produce visionary works – thoughts and ideas. They are self-taught, or self-*thought*, individuals working outside the religious mainstream.

Our very first formally-cited forebear, Michael Servetus, transgressed his society's bounds by questioning the Doctrine of the Trinity. In 1531, society deemed such thinking not "visionary" but "heretical" and it responded by burning Servetus at the stake. Hard to be more "outsider" than that!

Closer to our own time, our venerated Ralph Waldo Emerson started as an insider, a clergyman in the 19th-century Unitarian Church. He became a champion outsider, though, by renouncing his (still largely Christian-based) Unitarian ministry to develop his vision of Transcendentalism, which even 150 years ago presaged much of our 21$^{st}$- century naturalistic thinking. His good friend, Henry David Thoreau, while not a card-carrying Unitarian, was certainly a close fellow traveler. Spending much time alone in his Walden cabin, Thoreau lived literally as well as figuratively on society's fringe. He had scant use for steeples and saints, but he widened the perimeters of religion to encompass dirt and trees, a bird, a squirrel.

Not all outsider Unitarians have fled society. Indeed, Thomas Jefferson led the entire young American nation as its third President (succeeding, by the way, its second President, Unitarian John Adams). However, stung by charges that he was an "atheist, deist or devil," Jefferson perhaps thought it prudent to remain a nominal member of

90

his local Episcopal church, while confiding to a friend he would be "an Unitarian by myself." And barely 50 years ago, Unitarian Adlai Stevenson also ran for president. But his ruminative intellect inspired only a new pejorative, "egghead," and he was rejected not once but twice by the American society he sought to lead.[*] A long list of Unitarian social reformers, from Margaret Sanger to Whitney Young, have at once stood outside of, yet immersed themselves in the societies they tried to reform. As gadfly outsiders, they pushed and prodded their societies to embrace their visions of greater justice and equality.

Imagining such company has made me feel less isolated in my solitude. I may or may not have some form of conventional artistic abilities, but I am proud to count myself among the Unitarian Universalist outsider artists of the spirit.

---

[*] At the risk of breaching neutrality, I confess my consternation at the apparent *appeal* of George W. Bush's anti-intellectualism.

# INTERESTING TIMES

A somber "Sharing" one Sunday reflected a week of dark personal developments for us at SUUS. During coffee, I remarked on this to Scott Liell, who replied diplomatically that, yes, it had been an "interesting" week. I trotted out my well-worn (threadbare?) line that the wish for someone to live in interesting times was an old Chinese curse. Scott was surprised: "Oh? I always thought it was a Chinese blessing." True to one of my less admirable traits, I was quick to set him straight and assure him that, of course, my version was correct, period. But he got me to (re)thinking. . . .

Among my collected quotes (the Smithsonian will get my by-now famous file folder after I pass my expiration date) is a touchstone thought from writer Haywood Hale Broun: "There will come a time when passion is gone. There will come a time when ambition is gone. Curiosity will sustain you." Having lost passion and never having had much ambition anyway, I am still diverted and sustained each day by my enduring curiosity about what is new to me, what is unusual, unexpected, extraordinary. Life is just so tumultuously and, yes, *blessedly* interesting.

I drive to work one morning and pass a formerly staid house where suddenly not one but 25 or 30 plastic pink flamingos perch on single metal legs all over the front lawn. A flock migrating to Disney World's fantasyland? An underpass takes me beneath I-95 and I glimpse a wooden house being towed on a flatbed trailer, but from my looking-up perspective all I can see is a log cabin tooling down the highway by itself.

Occasionally, I shelve books in the Guilford Library, outwardly "to aid the community," but perhaps more to turn loose this little boy in a candy store of interesting things by the shelf load. In the language section, there are, of course, the Spanish and French dictionaries, but you can also select beginning grammars to teach yourself Icelandic or Egyptian. With the structure-of-matter texts, there is also a book on the physics of soap bubbles. In fact, if you define "God" as whatever force(s) brought the Universe into being, and you grant that physicists' interest in solving this ultimate puzzle completely consumes them, then I can be quite comfortable picturing a physicist as the object of the Psalmist's rhapsody, "His delight is in the law of the Lord; and in his law doth he meditate day and night."

But what of those dark, bad things to which the "curse" reading of the phrase sardonically refers? Well, the sculptor Louise Nevelson, for example, was once displeased with the design of a chair. However, her comment was, "You know, that chair's not so hot... but look at its shadow!" Psychotherapist Viktor Frankl, imprisoned in a Nazi concentration camp, took soul-saving interest in a bird that landed near him once in the field of mud where he toiled. And American icon Ozzie Nelson regarded his final illness with a stoic wonderment. A non-smoker with lung cancer, he remarked, "Isn't that interesting?" The narrator of a traditional blues song lists all his life's trials and disasters, yet still decides, "The only reason I stick around at all is just to see what's gonna happen next."

So the trick, apparently, is to *interpret* bad times as "interesting" nonetheless. Adopt that perspective and no matter what life has hidden just around the corner, that Chinese invocation will always be a blessing.

## SECULAR AND SACRED

Twenty years ago, in one of the subset of "mini-lives" that comprise the whole of my life's trek so far, I took a job as the baker in a funky, small restaurant off the Guilford Green. Any lunch specials left after two days on the counter became help-yourself fodder for the kitchen crew. Soon, I was regularly taking home succulent things like wild rice salad and fresh chicken salad with toasted pecans. I felt that I had landed with, to airbrush an Irish expression of my mother's, "my posterior in a butter tub." But after a month or two, I began to regard this largess

with, "Oh, hum, wild rice salad *again*?" Today, as I daily bless each leaf of green cabbage or cup of black coffee, that attitude quite embarrasses me. I see it as the outlook of some corpulent, debauched Nero.

Thirty-eight years ago, I moved from the New Jersey town where I grew up to my new home in Guilford, Connecticut.

I was happy to be transplanting my life here because from the time I was five years old, New England had been my cherished annual vacationland. On a midweek spring morning, I drove up I-95 to take ownership of the new home. At Darien, I looked off the highway to my left and saw the white spire of a church thrusting above the tops of leafing trees. A common sight hereabouts, but to me, the image was powerful, iconic. It signaled a welcome to me and told me this new home was no ordinary place but was, indeed, my own promised land. Four decades later, I still behold any church spire as a reminder that I'm not "just" in Branford or Clinton, but that I'm in a hallowed place, my New England.

Conversely, a return visit once to my childhood New Jersey home proved an even more powerful experience. During an hour's sojourn in Ridgewood, I wanted to see again the house I lived in from age five through twenty-two – that is, if it was still standing. My breaths came quicker as I drove into Eton Court (a baseball diamond for us Court kids) and beheld "my" house, completely renovated but still there. I got out of the car and to the present owner, out front tending the lawn, I explained who I, a stranger, was. To my delight – and trepidation – she invited me in. The interior seemed Lilliputian – had small dolls once lived here? – and its mundane spaces filled my eyes with tears. The bedroom where my bunk bed once held me. The bathroom tub – the *bathtub*, dear God! I once soaked in that tub and played with my toy pirate ship. I felt strange relief that the renovation had eliminated my parents' bedroom. On entering that room that long-ago Christmas Eve morning, I confronted the curled, bedridden body of my father, mercifully dead after a horrific illness. Had the room been there to enter again, I truly thought that I might faint.

In Thornton Wilder's "Our Town," young Emily dies in childbirth but is granted a return visit to Earth for one day. She is overcome with emotion by every "ordinary" thing. She realizes that every space is sacred, every object hallowed, simply by its very existence in this living world. I try to remember this with every mundane chore I undertake. Not to mention with every wild rice salad I eat.

# WHAT LASTS

A recent day off from work took me into New Haven to view a Frank Lloyd Wright exhibit at the Yale School of Architecture. Regrettably, I seem never to catch a day off from the ponderous musings of my own mind, and a stroll along York Street on a sunny spring day turned into a rumination on permanence and loss. Permanence and the quest for what, if anything, lasts – these are spiritual matters for me. I yearn for a spiritual Rock – something granite-solid I can lean my soul against, knowing it will never give way on me.

Just before the Architecture School, I came upon an empty lot. Immediately, I recalled what once stood here: a one-story building that housed a clothing store called Gentree's. I envisioned that if I walked backwards down the block and could walk backwards through 30-odd years in time, I would return to the winter day I entered Gentree's to buy a coveted gray sheepskin coat. I cherished its timelessly stylish lines and I thought its high-collared snugness would keep me warm through generations of wear. Now the coat remains in my closet where it has hung, unworn, for a decade or two. Wearing it, I discovered its snug fit actually constricted normal movement. Besides, I've changed; I don't – won't – wear animal skins anymore and I'd be embarrassed to be seen in it. My coat for a lifetime didn't last.

The clothing store didn't last either. At some point, the coats and trousers were carted out, professional stoves, exhaust fans and tables and chairs were carried in, and the space became Gentree's restaurant. Twenty-odd years ago, my former partner, Nancy, and I enjoyed occasional all-you-can-eat BBQ rib nights there. But food pleasures changed. Now I seldom eat meat – rarely pork and never beef – nor trans-fatted French fries either.

Nor did our love, a potentially permanent human experience, last. It happened to evolve into something alternate, and now we carry on an affectionate correspondence over a distance of four states. But I regret that the loving relationship Nancy and I enjoyed on those nights at Gentree's is past.

And now I stood and saw that even the Gentree's building was gone. I had read that architects are egotists who regard their edifices as permanent monuments to their lives on Earth. Tell it to the builders of Penn Station, the World Trade Center ... and Gentree's.

Whoa, I was digging my gloom hole pretty deep. It was then that I had my Buddhist/Viktor Frankl moment. I glanced down the block at a cluster of daffodils I had just passed and remembered this trip was supposed to be fun. Viktor Frankl said we can choose to experience either the joy or despair latent in each moment we live, and I determined to reclaim this moment's joy. I realized that this present moment was followed by a next moment with its own potential for joy or despair, then by another next moment and on and on, creating what someone (the Buddha? Freud? No matter) called "the eternal now" where we spend our entire lives. The *eternal* now – it *lasts*. Intellectually, we nod acceptance of the fact that we will die, but I think we secretly agree with William Saroyan who said he always thought in his case "an exception would be made." We live as if our now moments will *forever* last. Now is what we have. It must be enough.

# THAT (OTHER) MAN

A papyrus scroll unearthed and carbon dated circa one (month) BMG – Before Mel Gibson

I have long considered myself an attitudinal scion of our prickly, yet cherished late member, Lois Lowell. While not as forthright – or courageous – as Lois, I see myself as she was – a respectful dissenter, often differing with the majority opinion, even among us SUUS mavericks. Never a "yes man," I see myself more as a "yes, but..." man. Thus cast, I share my reservations about a putatively revered figure: "that (other) man," Jesus.

I'm told (I was born in 1946) that some of the generation preceding mine referred, not admiringly, to Franklin Roosevelt as *"that man,"* usually punctuated with an exclamation point of exasperation. UUs have traditionally professed (paid lip service to?) an esteem for, if not worshipful reverence of, Jesus as one of history's great spiritual teachers. A 1959 Guide to Unitarianism said, "Religion is a universal experience. Jesus of Nazareth is to be seen as one of the great exemplars of this universal religion. [His words] were true and beautiful." Oh? Various words attributed to Jesus grate harshly against my UU ideals of tolerance and inclusiveness, and make me think he is equally deserving of the FDR pejorative.

Today, we are fond of quoting that "love is the spirit of this church." But the Gospels record Jesus as saying to skeptics of his preaching, "Ye serpents, ye generation of vipers, how can ye escape the damnation of hell," and "Whosoever speaketh against the Holy Ghost it shall not be forgiven him neither in this World nor in the world to come." This scarcely manifests love and tolerance toward those of different mind. Perhaps Jesus, like us on

Sundays, might have benefited from a Q&A discussion after his sermons. Moreover, the idea of God condemning some people to eternal punishment after life is the very concept in opposition to which Universalists first coalesced as a denomination. Universalists defined themselves by contending that a loving God (or son of God) would never do such a thing, and that salvation was "universal."

In another famous (notorious?) passage, Jesus is equally condemning of the man who has committed adultery in his heart as he is of the man who has actually done the deed. This equation of private thought with overt act has contorted countless minds over the centuries with self-destructive guilt. And what human being has *never* regarded another person either yearningly or feloniously? In Jesus' eyes, we're *all* guilty of adultery or manslaughter.

Fortunately for civil liberties, however, our nation's laws include the premise that you are innocent until proven guilty of some actual, physical commission of a crime, that bad intentions are not enough (though lately it's getting a little harder to rest easy about this). Jesus' views would throw us on the mercy of George Orwell's thought police, or the "pre-crime" police (of the movie "Minority Report") who arrested people for crimes contemplated, not committed. Maybe this is a reason John Ashcroft so admires Jesus.

So, after all, I believe Jesus was certainly not God on Earth, but an imperfect, mortal human being like us all.

## PRECIOUS LORD (THERAPIST, BROKER, ET AL.) TAKE MY HAND

Blame it – so fashionable nowadays – on my faulty upbringing, at once neglected as well as overly sheltered. A rare 1950s child of divorce, I spent many solitary after-school afternoons withdrawing from the company of the born-again fundamentalist matron who babysat me. No surprise, she was not my intimate confidant and I was occasionally the captive audience for impromptu sermons by her street corner-preacher husband. Before the split, my parents deflected my questions about the – sad – realities of the world. I asked why a political cartoon about the Korean War "wasn't funny"; they said, "You'll understand when you're older." They may have wished not to add to an already-evident puerile angst, but the result of their well-intended protection was that I didn't even know how to write a bank check until I was twenty-one years old.

All my (heh) adult life, I've felt like a teetering infant reaching for any parental hands to steady and guide me. That this may not be solely *my* analyst's couch issue came to me via a New Yorker cartoon where a man enters a cocktail party. His hair stands on end and his thought balloon exclaims, "Yipes! Grown-ups!" Corroboration that I'm not alone in this yearning came from a book review of "The Road to Delphi: The Life and Afterlife of Oracles," which chronicles "our longing for certainty and our insatiable appetite for signs and omens" from the ancient Greek gods to New Age tarot card readers. In this wired, digital world, we may all feel a bit in over our heads and in need of a guiding elder – hence tech support personnel, financial advisors, psychiatrists – and ministers.

I left off to go cook supper. At least in the kitchen I feel sufficiently confident to no longer need cookbooks to guide me along. I diced a potato and sautéed it in a pan. I'd intended simply to add some sliced onion and shredded cheddar. Then I saw the can of water chestnuts on the shelf. Suddenly, I replaced the cheese with the chestnuts, adding also some soy sauce, ginger, carrot strips and chopped peanuts. My unanticipated dish so pleased me that I even replaced my fork with chopsticks.

As I ate, I reflected that when I write these essays, as well, I often wind up in a place rather different from where I began to go. I *can* be my own – unexpected – helmsman. Recent additions to my by-now famous quotes file came flooding back to me. Artist William Steig said he worked best when he didn't know what he was going to do, and architect Frank Gehry said, "If you know where it's going, it's not worth doing." Painter Romare Bearden said, "You should never be too sure of where you want to go, because it would be too easy to get there."

Besides, thinking back forty years ago recently, I considered the futility of many best-laid plans anyway. As his open Continental limousine rolled into Dealey Plaza, JFK may well have been preoccupied with how his waves and Jackie's smiles would benefit his upcoming '64 re-election strategy. He needn't have worried.

I found this notion of surrendering guidance to trust (Faith?) most gracefully phrased by author E. L. Doctrow. He commented, "Writing [and, I would add, life itself] is like driving at night with the headlights on. You can only see a few feet in front of you, but you can make the whole journey that way."

# SLAVES

Over what has now become years (!) of writing these things, I have focused almost exclusively on personal experience and anecdote, dwelling at times on minutiae. Feeling more than sufficiently challenged trying to reflect on, perhaps (perhaps!) make sense of my own life, I have shied away from commenting on any larger issues. The title "For What It's Worth" was meant to convey the uncertainty with which I undertook this project. However, recently I watched a public television show that sufficiently stirred my heart (as, I fear, few things seem able to do anymore) to make me want to write about it.

The program was a history of slavery in this land that became the United States of America, from the earliest colonial settlements up to our Civil War. It wrapped itself around me personally for two reasons: it portrayed on a national level that quality of self-contradiction, of saying one thing and doing another, that has long perplexed me when I see it on the personal, individual level; and it further

cleaned from my glasses a rose color, through which I used to view race reality.

Twenty years ago, when I was a capital-F Foodie, I smiled at wine critics' quip that people "talked dry but drank sweet"; they claimed to *appreciate* a crisp-dry Chablis but they snuck off to buy their pink, fizzy-sweet Riunite. Currently, in our Time of the Scandal, people profess to be weary of sordid news, but *somebody's* buying all those Stars and Enquirers, *somebody's* keeping two Clinton/Lewinsky books on the best seller lists.

Fudging on what you drink or read is of little consequence, but the TV show profiled our Founding Fathers as Janus-faced regarding the high ideals on which they based this nation. George Washington and Thomas Jefferson came under a particularly leveling, clear-eyed gaze. Washington, the "father of his country," was also "the *owner* of 300 human beings." Jefferson wrote the very words, "All men are created equal," while his personal slave waited in the same room to fulfill his any wish. Certain of Jefferson's writings on race sounded more like they came from Sheriff Bull Conner than from our Unitarian icon, hero of my adolescence. The Fathers based their entreaties to Britain for independence on the idea that humans have a natural right to be free; identical appeals written to *them* by educated slaves were rejected. Ah, but "nothing is harder to become than the person you always claimed to be."

As a child, I accepted as perfectly reasonable my parents' instruction to be respectful of and polite to other people. By age 10, I had rejected my Sunday School Protestantism, predicated on accepting Jesus as some supernatural being. So when, at 17, I discovered UUism, a faith predicated on respecting the dignity and worth of every person, I could accept it too as "perfectly reasonable," the answer to this agnostic's prayers. In 1962, respect for individuals also seemed to me to be the reasonable (read naive) answer to the civil rights ferment then swirling our country. All we had to do was hold hands, sing "We Shall Overcome" and all be friends. Even in the early '90s, I still found myself seconding Rodney King's plaintive (read simplistic) question. Shaken by the violence that followed the (all white) jury's acquittal of the police who beat him, he faced news cameras and asked, "Why can't we all just get along?"

Well, the TV program detailed for six grim hours reasons why, even these hundreds of years later, we still cannot "just get along". Generation after generation of lives were lived in fear and anger at having one's family unity, health, safety – one's very *life* – all dangling at the whims of one's owner – *owner!* A generation, even a century, may be too short a time to cast off a legacy that heavy. Thich Nhat Hanh said, "This is like this because that is like that." Regarding that terrible subjugation institutionalized in the nation he helped create, Thomas Jefferson wrote, presciently, "If God is just, we will pay for this." Sir, we're still paying.

# NOTHING LASTS – GOOD!

During Sharing one Sunday, I cited a letter in (where else?) the Sunday Times Book Review that questioned the appeal of some popularly held concepts of "Heaven." The writer was skeptical of the cloying sweetness of the supposed place, in William Jame's phrase, "the atrocious harmlessness of all things." He also mused on whether Heaven's endless pleasures *are* pleasures after all, and not just tedium. This notion prompted in me examples to suggest that "Heaven" isn't something eternal, but rather consists of fleeting moments whose very briefness makes them more rewarding and "heavenly."

My commute to work is highlighted by drive-by glimpses of two enchantingly gnarled trees; their serpentine branches are nothing less than poems in wood. It came to me that the reason they divert me daily is, indeed, the abbreviated view I get of them. I can behold them for only three or four seconds before I would steer the car into oncoming traffic or off the road. I fear that should I ever just stop the car, get out and walk around them for an hour, then the next day they'd be just two more trees in the forest.

Years ago, I was the baker at a small Guilford restaurant. With my waste-abhorring New England soul, I replaced the dumpster as the final resting place for plats du jour too old to offer again in the Café but too young for salmonella. I was, as it were, in pig heaven … for a week or two. But after a month of poached salmon and wild rice doggie bags, I descended back to earth. My haute cuisine leftovers had become just … leftovers.

I would even be so bold as to venture an inch or so onto the lethally thin ice of discussing relationships. If marriages are made in heaven, then why do statistically half of them fail? Does not familiarity breed, well, if not contempt, then at least ordinariness? "I'd give anything to spend Saturday night with that person" is a different prospect from, "Gee, I think I'll spend the rest of my life with that person."

Well, what about one of the most enduring of pleasures: music? Imagine the appeal (?) of endless celestial harp concertos. Classical music is by definition of lasting, even endless appeal, but is it? Granted, Beethoven wears better than Madonna, but is there anyone who doesn't have to *work* at fresh enthusiasm for, say, the opening of the fifth Symphony? Oooohh! … *another* da-da-da-*duh* ?! And if we are to find Handel without end gratifying, not stultifying, then who made the timid harp the instrument of choice? I recall the Gary Larson cartoon: on one half of a split-screen frame, new arrivals in Heaven are greeted, "Welcome to Heaven. Here's your harp." On the other side, those entering Hell are told, "Welcome to Hell. Here's your accordion." In these world-beat, zydeco-rockin' times, maybe those instruments have now been switched.

*Anything* endless seems to overlook two true things. One I might call a truth of contrasts. Without something opposite, pleasure has no meaning. A draught of cool water is not refreshing to those who have never been thirsty; heat holds no comfort for those who have never been cold. And the culinary cliché is right; variety *is* the spice of life. Without the cayenne sting of some adversity, life would be as zesty as a bowl of unseasoned cream of wheat.

Jean-Paul Sartre wrote a play called "No Exit", about characters trapped somewhere that had "no exit," no way out – a situation that had no end. You can guess where they were. Hint: it wasn't Heaven.

## ... AND A LITTLE CHILD SHALL ...

I was intrigued by the concepts explored in a PBS series on the brain: how we get and keep *trillions* of pieces of information in a space the size of a grapefruit. But after an hour of brain-wave charts and flash-card test reenactments, my interest flagged. I felt the frustration of Dylan Thomas as a child in Christmastime Wales whose didactic book gift told him everything about the wasp – except why.

I had read that the series' producer previously avoided such programs because "Lost in a proliferating thicket of questions, I was never able to find my way back to that initial curiosity and wonder that inspired the investigation in the first place." Amen. When I was seven or eight, I would wander my backyard, lie in the grass, watch bugs, gaze at the sky. My mind was making wild, random leaps, wondering wild, random questions. Nearly five decades later, those same preoccupying reveries are still the main business of my day.

Leaving for work recently, I was aware of how my brain routinely functions on two levels:

1.) Start car. Need gas yet? What's today? When fill tank, buy milk too? Check mileage. Should change oil by, say, March. Remember to buy filter. See mailbox across the road. Must write check for phone bill – due Friday. Sun fading behind clouds. These shoes right for the predicted rain?

2.) Pull out of garage to be underneath the sky. Wow – look at those big puffy, muscular clouds – dark purple! – ganging up on the very

111

Sun! The Smiths' blinds are up; I can see that neat model sailboat in their window. Ooops – there's their tri-color cat, Elle, in the window too. Don't knock that boat over, pussycat! I love their crouching gargoyle garden statue – similar stone demons are scowling down on Paris from Notre Dame's buttresses right this minute. Hmmm, a wind's making those bushes wave; they look like they're underwater. Well, I guess we all live on the bottom of this air ocean, just as lobsters live on the water ocean bottom.

Admittedly, this brain activity hasn't made me CEO material. And like Ferdinand the Bull, I've never been driven by machismo to play the determined, aggressive male. But that's okay; my role models have always been more Thoreau and Johnny Appleseed than Donald Trump and Attila the Hun.

Maybe I'm some example of arrested development whose child-mind attention span never achieved an adult level of sometimes lengthy commitment to enterprise. Maybe that's why I'm more passionate about SUUS services, where we gather weekly to metaphorically lie in the grass and wonder about Things, than I am about the gritty workaday world where middle age has presently plunked me. I am grateful that the Universe has been gentle with me as I've meandered my way through 55 years so far. Lucky for me God protects fools and little children – I think I could qualify for both.

I can't say I recommend my desultory ways as a career strategy – tuitions and mortgages too expensive these days. As an occasional indulgence of the spirit, however, childlike reverie ain't half bad. It can make leaving for work a lot more agreeable.

# A MINOR ESSAY: LIFE, ART, MEANING, GOD

In a lake near my house sits a large rock. This boulder slopes up to a Gibraltar apex, and when seen with its mirror opposite reflected on the water, the double image looks like a giant oyster. In fact, I have replaced its reality with my artful perception. I think of it not as "my rock,"but as "my oyster." Indeed, by glancing around my New England town the way a film director frames shots with his joined thumbs and index fingers, I have abstracted the reality of local streets and fields into "lost paintings" to accompany cherished works of Andrew Wyeth and Edward Hopper.

Why do we humans have this urge to turn life into art? I believe this Universe we live in is completely random, neutral and without judgment. My rock is not really a mollusk except that I metaphorically – artistically – call it so. It is not beautiful nor ugly, certainly not good nor bad; it simply "is." In fact, it's not even a "rock" except that someone named it so.

Through art, we bring order to rhymeless, random reality. A meadow is unfettered; out of it we make an arrangement of wildflowers, in a bowl or on a canvas. We orchestrate random tones into the Ninth Symphony. Out of our chaotic thoughts and emotions we make compositions: "Beowulf" and "King Lear." With art, we also give human *meaning* to the neutral "is-ness" we exist in. Claude Monet is "serenity"; Jackson Pollack is "agitation." The Ninth Symphony is "triumph;" "Othello" is "jealousy."

This bringing of order and meaning seems necessary – vital – to our human life. I recall a futuristic movie where society's worst punishment was to banish a person to an endless, barren white void with no floor,

115

ceiling, perimeter or horizon. And, except that it's black, not white, and punctuated with rocks and gases, is not our Universe the same meaningless void? Perhaps our religions are our attempts to bring order and meaning to this ultimate emptiness. Thus our artistic stories of Creation and Creator, of Jehovah and Brahma, of "Let there be light" and Turtle Island. This art of our religions also gives us a sense of control in our Universe. If we forgo this meat, imbibe this wine or bow in a certain direction, then all will be well.

And who am I to naysay such a sense of well-being as that which our religions bring to so many? Whether our myriad beliefs comport with reality or are our artistic creations is not arguable. If they make our lives easier, what can be bad? Besides, who knows but that there may reside some Creator in the folds and crinkles of time as yet unrevealed to us. As they say in certain circles, "If the Sox can win the Series..." anything can happen.

# A MODEST NOTION

By this time (summer 2005 will mark 10 years of your allowing me this page to navel-gaze and vent) I often feel that I'm simply recycling the thoughts I've gleaned from my latest library book or Sunday paper article. I console (justify?) myself that even Will Rogers claimed to know only what he read in the papers, and Mark Twain said, "Adam was the only man who, when he said a good thing, knew that nobody had said it before him."

But now and then, my quirky-jerky brain synapses seem to synthesize disparate readings into something with a whiff of freshness to it. My outsider original opinions may one day get me escorted away by stern and strong-armed men. While certainly not fearless, at least heedless of such consequence, I record here one such modest opinion.

For some months, I've harbored a perhaps peevish reluctance to reconcile myself to the 2004 election outcome and the Fundamentalist Nation demographic it reflected. In reaction, I've lately read several restatements of the argument that humans, indeed, created God and not the other way around. One book, "The End of Faith," even says out loud that our clashing, obdurate beliefs in a supernatural God have become a lethal anachronism in our terror-wracked world, and must be discarded, as were the Greek myths and medieval superstitions.

I've also read recently that Google (*absurd* name, no?!) has made the books of several major world libraries available to all on the Internet. This seems to me the latest marker knot in a line stretching back through Diderot's Encyclopedists clear back to the Library of Alexandria and even, metaphorically, to the Bible short story of the tower of Babel, intended to reach Heaven itself. I think all these

117

endeavors reflect a defining characteristic of humans: our urge, our quest to find out and record all there is to know – to become omniscient, *god-like*. Human history can be seen as one long activity of discovery – finding out the next fact geographically, scientifically, culturally. Plato commented, "Nothing is; everything is becoming."

But at some point, the Catch-22 of this grand enterprise becomes apparent. What if someday we *do* discover every last thing and know All There Is? Why, then the game is up; there would be nothing left to do, and we humans would just as well pack up our tent and go home – as in *cease to exist any longer*.

So, perhaps we created "God" to insure against our own self-extinction. We fabricated some being, some power that gave order to atomic nuclei and Horse Head nebula, something that *was* before Creation's first second and still *will be* after its last moment. On purpose, we imagined something so limitless and overwhelming that we could *never* figure it out. For us to fathom "God" would be less likely than for a cockroach scurrying through Times Square to master the mechanics, technology, sociology and metaphysics of the buildings, signs, taxis and tourists that towered above it. Thus did we perpetuate ourselves. And, though like Dan Quale, I may be accused of conflating reality and fiction, I'd venture that thwarting the tower of Babel could've been the biggest favor God ever did us.

Herewith ends the modest notion for today. Cue those strong-armed men if you wish; Mr. DeMille, I'm ready for my close-up.

# BELIEFS: MINE, YOURS AND THE TRUTH

"Rich, the parent corporation took away from us a major part of our business, and we're forced to make cutbacks. I regret to tell you that we're terminating your employment with us as of today."

These words punched me in the face. My thoughts staggered. All the planets in my orderly universe spun wildly out of their fixed orbits. No Biblical scholar, I can't claim that passages from Job sprang to my mind, but I did find my feelings corroborated in the laments of that fable's afflicted soul when I consulted my King James: "I will speak in the bitterness of my soul. I will say unto God ... shew me wherefore thou contendest with me." "Terrors are turned upon me ... my welfare passeth away as a cloud." "… the days of affliction have taken hold upon me."

*What*, dear reader may query, was Rich Gressley doing with his nose stuck in a Bible? I was discovering that, like foxholes, unemployment as well knows no agnostic/atheists (yours truly). To explain my sudden misfortune, I sought Reasons – supernatural, epistemological, eschatological, cabalistic or otherwise. I became a subscriber to a variety of notions: that my romanticized feminine God, who has always been gentle with me, simply lifted me out of my rut to infuse more Life into my life; that a "help wanted" sign at an admired store that I passed the day after my layoff meant that, of course, *this* would be my next job; that encountering a favorite past colleague working at another place I applied to meant, of course, that *that* would be my next job...

Adversity can be better borne if an explanation for it can be found – or invented. But part of me – the part that occupies a seat at SUUS on Sunday mornings, was uncomfortable with this magical thinking. It seemed an example of "post hoc, ergo propter hoc" reasoning – "after this, therefore because of this." A shaman does a rain dance, then it rains. Thus his dance made it rain. Well... maybe.

More consonant with my gut feelings is the belief that, as UU minister Kenneth Patton titled one of his books, "Man [is] the Meaning Maker." In the eponymous movie, Lawrence of Arabia voices his belief with the line, "Nothing 'is written' unless I write it." As Kierkegaard said, "Life can only be understood backward, but it must be lived forward." Sometimes, meaning making is a group effort; one of our hymns says that as we weekly live our lives, then "we come together here [at SUUS] to make sense of what we find." And if our meaning stories are not 100% accurate, well ... that's all right. Poet A. R. Ammons, feeling " there's so much more belief than truth," tells us "all in all, the world doesn't make much sense unless we make up a little something to go with it."

Our beliefs are our spiritual placebos. This is no disparagement. In medicine, patients given sugar pills they were told were potent drugs have shown dramatic improvement. Likewise, it matters not so much that our personal beliefs coincide with objective (whatever *that* is) truth, but that we think they do. If we espouse the truth of our personal beliefs – and deciding for ourselves what our beliefs are is one of UUism's highest charges to us –then our spiritual placebos may go far to remedy our existential maladies.

# EATING, READING, BECOMING

"You are what you eat." As often as I've read culinary philosopher Brillat-Savarin's aphorism, I've never quite understood what he meant. If this were literally true, I would have morphed long ago into a head of cabbage, an onion or a bowl of ice cream, three of my most – dare I say? – consistently consumed comestibles. However, the only way these foods are manifest in me is that – how do I avoid indelicacy? – at certain times during the day, it would be imprudent to stand directly next to me. No, that can't be it. The ancient Romans believed you took on the character traits of the foods you ate. Thus, eating rabbit would make you timid; eating wolf (and they did!) would make you ferocious. I would probably characterize myself as timid, but from eating rabbit? While I confess to the meat-abstinent that I dearly love rabbit, still I can't remember how many years it's been since I partook of that tastes-like-chicken delicacy. According to theory, I should more closely resemble tenacious, upstream-battling salmon, which I do eat frequently – healthy, omega-3 oils, don'cha know. But, while I do exhibit a stubborn streak on occasion, I am not known for any do-or-die perseverance, and I hate cold water.

But "you are what you read" – now *there's* a truism. Lately, this came home to me as I combed my clipping files in search of a (still!) missing poem. I was powerfully struck by how much of what I consider the essence of *me* is made from those saved words. But as I widened this thought, the obviousness of it became shiningly apparent. Don't we all have favorite writers – novelists, philosophers, etc. who have influenced us and whom we quote? Aren't our political views molded in part by editorial writers in journals we respect and look to for guidance?

In fact the whole course of world history has been steered by persons who became what they read. How many economies have been shaped, how many wars fought by leaders who absorbed the words of Karl Marx? More fortuitously, we hope, the course of our nation has been guided by some who digested the writing of Thomas Jefferson, who in turn digested the writing of John Locke. For better (Martin Luther King Jr.) or for worse (Jerry Falwell), America has also been shaped by many who tried to embody the words attributed to, if not written by, Jesus.

But whole tomes are not for miniaturist me; too much bulk to stick to my small-boned ribs. Never have I slogged through the entire Bible, nor Gibbon nor Proust. Rather, my files are composed of a paragraph here, a single sentence there copied as a record of all that mattered to me

from entire books I've read. These compacted nuggets of thought are like molecules that, all together, make up the body of what I facetiously call "the man I am today."

Some thoughts I've absorbed into my very marrow: "Life can only be understood backwards, but it must be lived forward," and "Love is what happens to two people who don't know each other." These I've been known to espouse from my Richard Gressley soapbox. Others are attitudinal goals yet to be achieved: "If we are to dream, the flatteries of hope are as cheap, and pleasanter, than the gloom of despair." I try to keep straight which is already me and which is yet to be, for "Nothing is harder to become than the person you always claimed to be," or as Shakespeare put it, "If to do were as easy as to know what 'tis right to do."

Recently, I copied a new quote that resonated with my eating disordered life: "Much of our life is encoded in – and determined by – tiny, repetitive, deceptively trivial decisions about what we will and won't eat." While I think that sketches me aptly, I feel it also offers me a challenge to overcome the limitations it lays out. If I could transcend those limitations, I'd be happy to eat those words. Say, maybe *that's* what "you are what you eat" means.

# I THINK, THEREFORE I AM (TROUBLED)

When I was 19, I encountered a quote from UU minister Kenneth Patton that so impressed me I've kept it in my billfold ever since as "words to live by." It reads:

> "If when you see any one thing, you see it with the entire universe surrounding it, you have peripheral vision. If every moment you live is surrounded by all the past and all the future, you live in the religious sense of time. Religion is the total view."

This "think cosmologically, live locally" awareness seems to recur widely in UU thought. John Muir said you cannot pick up any one thing without discovering the whole Universe is attached to it. And Lydia Maria Child said (warned?) that once this awareness dawns, there is no turning back from it. Her words: "...I have lost the power of looking merely on the surface. Everything seems to me to come from the Infinite, to be filled with the Infinite, to be tending toward the Infinite."

It...*seemed* like a good idea. After all, UUs explain that our vaunted denomination is more than hoary stories retold and rote rituals reenacted one day a week. It is more of a total immersion, a way of living your entire life – 24/7, as current usage would have it. Many UUs feel an affinity for Buddhism, where this constant awareness of the larger context of one's daily activities is cultivated as "mindfulness."

Also, the UU history of social activism mirrors our awareness not only of the larger world's glories and beauty, but of its imperfections and inequities as well. A number in our movement have dedicated their lives to bettering myriad lamentable states of our being. Such lives are celebrated as well-spent, even noble.

But, jeez, don't we ever get a break? Mark Schenker told us how even Captain Ahab in "Moby Dick" confides to First Mate Starbuck his regret that, fixed on his higher purpose (killing the whale), he is no longer able to enjoy life's quotidian pleasures (Lydia Maria Child, take note). Earlier, Ahab threw his half-smoked pipe overboard since it no longer gave him enjoyment. This struck a chord (no pun intended) with this folkie who hadn't picked up his "cherished" Martin guitar in months. Mark then told us how Woody Allen reportedly attends N.Y. Knicks basketball games for relaxation, but when a Knick makes a basket, Woody's first thought is, "Someday, that man's going to be dead." More resonance with this SUUS congregant who can't enter our meeting room without recalling a litany of Those of Us Who Have Gone Before.

The high, cerebral road to spiritual attainment is strewn with nails. In a '50's submarine movie, actor Curt Jurgens had one memorable line: "You pay a penalty for thinking; you cannot rest." And polymath writer Diane Ackerman noted, with longing: "For a compulsively pensive person, to be fully alert but free of thought is a form of ecstasy." And, ironically, in Buddhism, for all its "mindfulness," the highest blessedness of Nirvana is a state of release from the care (read "thought") of the external world.

In a New Yorker cartoon, one physicist in the lab says to the other, "Sometimes I wonder if there's more to life than unlocking the mysteries of the Universe." Sure there is. It lies in the ability to (in my best approximation of 21st-century language) "kick back and chill out."

## OLLIE AND ME

I bled. I moaned. I complained to my listener one morning at church that my idea well for this page was fast running dry. Were the newsletter weekly instead of monthly, I'd have been out of print long ago. Fred Struve, who shall remain nameless, happens to be a booster of mine, for reasons best known to himself. He replied, "Just look around you and pick out something to write about. You have a way of seeing things that's different from other people." Uh … right.

At home later, my eyes sweeping around the living room stopped at a yellow upholstered rocking chair, in which I have not actually sat for years because it's really a pedestal for a favorite icon, my Oliver Hardy pillow. This beloved decorative throw is silk-screened with the bowler-

hatted face of the portly half of the comic duo Laurel and Hardy. Under that hat and some matted wisps of stringy hair (oh, yes, I identify!), he glowers in a scowl that holds in check – barely – an id rage at the absurd foibles of humankind. My guy!

With each year I age, my tolerance for people's quirks, mannerisms, pretensions and affronts (as perceived and so designated by yours truly) gets scraped ever thinner. To compound matters, my notoriously thin skin has lately been toiling behind the deli counter in a grocery store with an affluent clientele noted for its snooty condescension. The perfect storm conditions for me to *become* my Ollie-about-to-explode pillow. Or so, at least, it started out.

One sour-faced woman rejected my half-pound of sliced turkey breast as "too thickly cut," adding that I really should have known better. Waiting on her subsequently, I was civil – nothing more. One day, she asked for Lebanon bologna. Immediately, I recalled that dark, peppery-spicy sausage I enjoyed as a kid. I ventured, "Gosh, I haven't seen that in years…a Pennsylvania specialty, I think." The woman brightened for the moment. "Yes, I'm from Pennsylvania," she said. I returned, "My father was from Pennsylvania. York." "Oh. I don't know where that is." No matter. A gulf had been bridged. After that, I saw the woman not as sour, just kind of sad.

Another woman irritated me with her pouty distraction. Scant eye contact, never a "please" or "thank you" and her indecision as to what to order strained my patience in a job where speed is of the essence every minute of your eight-hour shift. Once, she came in wheeling a child in a carriage and wearing a T-shirt emblazoned with "Operation Gulf Storm" above a map of the Fertile Crescent. I overheard words of her conversation with the woman next to her: "husband … Marine … Iraq." I changed from thinking of her as "that pain of a woman" to "that woman in pain."

I recalled a contemporary folk song lyric: "There's a hole in the middle of the prettiest life…" And I remembered my own advice from a Sunday service I once gave on (of all things!) optimism. If someone's behavior irritates, even angers you, try *making up* some sympathetic story to explain it. It can't hurt and it might even be at least ballpark accurate.

I considered taking a magic marker to make Oliver Hardy's scowl a smirk, thus changing him from my "bad Buddha" into a "bemused Buddha." But no, I decided my friend Ollie should remain as he is; that's what makes him funny. Instead, I should more frequently upturn my own scowl into a trace smile, remembering a quality of the Buddha I'd overlooked – Buddha's pity.

# ABOUT THE AUTHOR

"For What It's Worth" is a collection of essays written over the past decade by Richard Gressley for the monthly newsletter of the Shoreline Unitarian Universalist Society, (SUUS) in Madison.

Gressley, a longtime member of SUUS, who had no previous writing experience and abhorred computers, first began writing the newsletter essays by hand in the spring of 1995, at the suggestion of Barbara Carlson, another SUUS member and a respected reporter for the Hartford Courant.

Born in Greenwich Village in lower Manhattan, Gressley moved across the Hudson with his parents when he was three years old, growing up in Ridgewood, New Jersey, where his first experience in organized religion was in the Sunday school of the local Dutch Reform Church. "After several years," he recalls, "I was chafing at Bible stories which I didn't put much stock in." His parents didn't object when he indicated he wanted out.

Later, he was exposed to a new religious movement when a classmate at Ridgewood High School invited him to attend a meeting of a youth group at the Ridgewood Unitarian Society. Soon afterward, in his senior year, he began attending the adult services with his father.

Gressley moved to the Connecticut shoreline in 1968, the year following the death of his father. One of his first priorities was to find a Unitarian church, which he did in the nearby town of Madison. SUUS was meeting on alternating Sundays in a town-owned building, the Madison Community House, the Rev. Mounir Sa'Adah serving as minister. The new congregation was first organized in March of 1962. It met earlier in private homes and the

Griswold House, a historic icon in neighboring Guilford, and was looking for a larger meeting area for a growing congregation that then numbered close to forty regulars.

Gressley was among the new members who moved in 1968 to its present location at 297 Boston Post Road, Madison. He remembers meeting in the crowded living room of the former private residence.

One of his first of many volunteer services was as chairman of the Sunday Services Committee, responsible for selecting and inviting a speaker for the next service.

While he had no experience in writing when it was suggested he do a monthly newsletter column, Gressley fell back on the foundation of his practice of self-education – reading. He had a voracious appetite for all kinds of reading – newspapers, magazines and good books. Among his early favorite authors – Nathaniel Hawthorne, Ralph Waldo Emerson, Herman Melville, Henry David Thoreau and Amy Lowell, all of them Unitarians.

Today Gressley continues each Sunday as the resident philosopher at SUUS, which now has close to 100 members – commenting on the latest essay in the New York Times, or making observations concerning a serious film offering or a magazine piece that struck his fancy and curiosity.

Richard Bastian
January 2009